Why the World Sucks

-

ISBN-13: 978-1500951382

ISBN-10: 1500951382

Why the World Sucks

TABLE OF CONTENTS

Chapter 1 – Our World Today

Most people have much to be thankful for, yet over a billion people barely survive in poverty. The answers to this and most of our national and global problems are already right under our noses. Whether our nation and world improves or survives depend to a great degree on the will of people to work toward positive changes to the existing system of things. It is not necessary to overthrow any government, economic system, culture, religion or philosophical ideas, but only to recognize the facts and to deal with them in constructive ways. As leaders and the populace stop seeking effective solutions to their collective problems, they continue to muddle in the mud where they've been stuck furthering senseless struggle that only causes them to sink deeper into the morass.

What are the major problems that confront our times that could lead to national and global economic meltdown, inhumane starvation and deaths, and more global wars? What are the solutions to solve the problems such as:

- Our national and global "economic cliff"
- National and global financial melt down
- Collapse of the international monetary system
- Massive unemployment
- Poverty and misery
- Environmental degradation beyond the "tipping point"
- Global warming
- Blood for oil wars
- Middle-East antagonism and extremism
- Overpopulation

- Nuclear proliferation
- Global thermal nuclear war?

Why do our world leaders continue to throw their hands up and present no new or effect solutions to long standing problems but instead continue to repeat all the tried and failed policies of the past? Real solutions begin with global leaders developing a shared vision of the world and international relations. The U.N. as a political forum should instead focus on humanitarian advocacy. Considering all the riches of the world, the vast majority of it still untapped (95%), why can't we have a world where basic human rights include:

- Adequate food and shelter
- Employment for those able to work
- An appropriate and applicable education
- Basic freedoms
- Protection from predators and criminals
- Entrepreneurial opportunities
- Minimal governmental red tape and obstruction

The most common human motivation has always been to seek a better life, to improve the immediate survivable environment in the hope it creates the circumstances for a better future not only for those living but for those yet to come. This has been a basic human emotion and desire that has been universal and has stood the test of time. Families and tribes have been built around this core value. Nations have risen or fallen as a consequence of the pursuit of this genetic predisposition – to better one's lot in life.

When governments become obstructionists, tyrannical or punitive in attempting to suppress this basic human desire, it's a matter of time perhaps within the span of several generations where the yoke of oppression is almost always overthrown. In response to oppression, history has shown that new political, financial and technological systems arise to foster greater opportunity for enlightenment and betterment. We now live in an instantaneous age where social media can spontaneously inspire massive responses to government and corporate policies. This has placed potentially unrestrained power back into the hands of the people as Arab Spring can attest during the Middle East uprisings during 2011.

Many of the topics and issues surrounding the betterment of our lives, our nation and that of the world have been discussed over the centuries in different perspectives responding to the concerns of their times. Several of the discussions contained in this compilation were first penned in 1995 while others were circa 2003, 2008 and more recently updated in 2012 as e-book publishing technology has made self publishing an affordable reality for heretofore unknown and unread authors.

It's the hope that some of the ideas contained in these essays will encourage readers to reflect, to think and to build improved lives for themselves, families, neighborhoods, nations and for the entire world. Many of the suggestions contained in these discussions have not been attempted on a large scale that is necessary for success as entrenched government and corporate elites prefer to continue milking the system for all its remaining juice even if it means leaving babies hungry and the poor dying in the streets. Shame on them. The other path is to seek constructive progress through a path of change that elevates humanity by exploring the abundance and not be limited by those who continue to hoard everything for themselves to the detriment of their nations and the global community.

Certainly the history of our world and nation has shown the ugly side of power, exploitation, oppression and the struggle for survival by the vast majority of people ever born. Even at the height of supposed highly enlightened, civilized and free nations in history, there existed the tale of two peoples, the privileged and powerful elite rich versus the forgotten poor and working classes. Almost all societies have been structured hierarchically to institutionalize the power, wealth and privileges of the elite classes to the detriment of the common people. That being said, must we accept that historical fact as the necessary foundation of future world civilizations where relatively few benefit as the vast majority of humanity suffers?

A world vision to better the lives of our nation and global communities must include at a minimum specific goals, including:

- A prosperous ecologically vibrant world at peace for all humans and living things.
- A vibrant global economy not slaves to price manipulation and wide market swings.
- Government's purpose as good stewards of their citizens' trust and well-being.
- National borders that are secure against terrorists and illegal immigration.
- Public officials who serve the public trust for public benefit and not for personal gain.
- Affordable high quality healthcare for all.

- Free or affordable pertinent quality education for those who want it.
- No one goes to bed hungry, especially children.
- Social consciousness that is respectful of ecology and
- conservation.
- Laws that are fair, egalitarian and just and not biased toward special interests.
- Affordable housing in safe neighborhoods for everyone.
- Positive incentives to reduce criminality, particularly for non-violent crimes.
- Sensible and ecologically sound development of land and natural resources.
- Improved matching of people to careers of their interests and passions.
- Preponderance of green energy to reduce dependency on fossil fuels.
- War as a last resort in dealing with tyrants who threaten world peace.
- Nuclear arms reduction to guarantee survival of the human race.
- Peaceful missions for the military-industrial complex, including space exploration.
- Population control to natural replacement levels, parents should not have children they don't plan to nurture and no more than the number they can reasonably afford.
- New cures for persistent diseases utilizing stem cell and genetic modification.

- Research to remove toxicity and harm from natural human vices.
- Tolerance for all religious beliefs up to the point they harm people and non-believers.

The world continues to be plagued by the constant threat of widespread warfare. Why can't we all just get along? Too often the conflicts that abound and surround nations and people's lives can be avoided or resolved by applying sensible attitudes toward each other, including:

- Fairness = Do unto others as you would have them do unto you. This requires the development of individual integrity, social conscience and compassion.
- Action to Reaction = There are consequences however large or small for every behavior and action that individuals, groups, organizations, corporations and governments take.
- Karma = Everything eventually comes around in principle whether good or bad where negative thoughts, speech and actions tend to create negative consequences and positive ones generally result in positive conclusions.
- Honesty = Dealing in facts rather than deception creates a climate of interaction that allows all parties the opportunities to see things for what they really are so conflicts can be resolved rather than exacerbated.
- Truth = There is no greater scientific and historical quest that pushes humanity forward.
- Freedom = If people are slaves to others whether in thoughts, emotions, physical needs, survival or governance, then better to fall into a deep sleep or coma.

- Justice = An eye for an eye. Now everybody knows the price for harming others. Steal a man's shirt, then one should become naked. Killing innocent people deserves death.
- Recovery = Where there is unequivocal and absolute proof of wrong doing by others well beyond suspicion, every person has a right to lawfully recoup their losses.
- Forgiveness = Once perpetrators are shown the evil of their ways, individuals may free their emotional trauma and hateful bondage simply through true forgiveness. However, they need not forgive if they prefer to exact justice, but forgiveness is often more effective and less painful in the long run.
- Deservedness = Everyone should receive what they earn whether it be credit, material gain, admiration, or punishment. Each individual is fully responsible for their personal thoughts, speech and actions and the consequences that follow.
- Kindness and Charity = It may require more personal sacrifice to be a giver, but were misfortune to befall anyone, it's gratifying to know others care and have kind hearts.
- Love and Compassion = What the world needs now, is love sweet love. No one chooses misfortune and suffering and those who show love and compassion do much to alleviate the misery that many go through in their struggle to survive.
- Open mindedness = No one can possibly know everything and history has shown again and again that apparent conventional wisdom, scientific theories and facts often times change as more knowledge is discovered.

- Questioning = It's not wise to accept anything at face value as a book's cover says little about its contents. A person's quest should be to understand themselves and their environment through inquiry rather than through group think, persuasion, or coercion.
- Acceptance = No one can honestly get everything they want and external forces often change our paths as people react and internalize ever changing life situations. If a river is stronger than one's ability to swim upstream, then the result would be the same as floating downstream with less struggle and effort. Sometimes we can only accept our situations and make the best of them.
- Random Luck = Nothing in life is preordained by genetics or environment. Things often happen for no apparent reason of ones choosing. People may call their fortunes or misfortunes as their fates, but randomness within a pattern of social structure is more often the limiting or modifying aspects of one's life path. Crap happens, but sometimes you get lucky. Sometimes life seems like a crap shoot, but every dog has its day. Does "genetic fate" really exists, or is it mostly up to the individuals?
- Wisdom = Everyone makes mistakes but only fools keep repeating them.
- Passion = When there isn't a strong desire for anyone, any cause, or anything, then life can feel awfully empty. Life can become a fake but secure shadow of reality.

- Personal Accomplishment = Look to oneself rather than to others to define what is worth achieving as no one else can truly look into another person's mind and heart to know for sure any more than self-motivated and honest people can know about themselves.
- Personal Responsibility = Own up to the direct and perhaps indirect consequences of personal speech, behaviors and actions – not claiming blameless when truly at fault, but also having the courage to resist accepting blame under coercion when innocent.
- Get the big picture = Know where one's life fits in to the scheme and structure of where they are at, the environment, people, situations, rules, norms, customs and whatever external forces can either limit or expand one's life experiences in positive or negative ways. No man is an island unto himself – and that goes for women too. Simply wanting or expecting something doesn't make it so. Do you really deserve it?

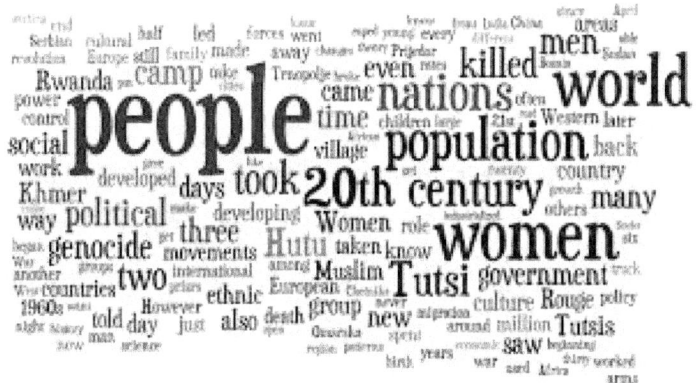

Chapter 2 – American Idealism

AMERICAN IDEALS are based upon compassion, benevolence, fairness and justice. Most of the world's peoples look to America, Americans and the American way of life for support, guidance and trends. But let's look at what is at the heart of what most Americans want as commonalities across almost all political parties, social class, race and gender? Let's list some of the fundamental ideas that bind Americans together as a culture:

- Financial security for their immediate needs and future
- Personal safety for themselves, family and friends
- Adequate housing, food and health care
- Basic Constitutional freedoms and liberties
- Honesty in government officials and bureaucrats
- Honesty in business, on Wall Street and among CEOs
- Opportunities to pursue personal happiness
- Personal responsibility vs. undeserved entitlements
- Fairness in all government dealings – transparency
- More discretionary income to pursue interests
- Minimally intrusive government on all levels
- Reduced special interest influence on government
- Smaller more efficient and effective government bureaucracy
- Less taxation and fees – spend wisely what you have
- Elected officials to tend to the people's business instead of partisanship

Americans and the world have witnessed the great American democratic electoral process in full swing in 2012, from its high points to its low. It has been depicted as an epic battle between the old politics of divisiveness versus a new change toward class, race, age and gender unity. However, the details of the call for change have been nebulous at best and often the proposed changes are little more than a minor redistribution of resources from the have lots to the have nots and have less. At the core of the broad variation in political stances lie the philosophical foundation of a progressive humanistic philosophy based upon a strong moral foundation founded in spiritual beliefs that has driven Americans both to great heights and also to win great wars.

While a healthy degree of skepticism abound in the general populace, notions of a better society and world remains the heartfelt hope of the vast majority of Americans from all walks of life. All people desire and are willing to struggle for a better life for themselves and their families. The struggle for survival, the contest between man and nature and the coexistence between the elites and the masses has been an endless cycle of ebb and flow in mankind's history. In the current socio-economic hierarchical paradigm, the rich get richer while the poor get poorer because the wealthy elites have institutionalized advantages over the working classes and poor whose consumerism actually holds up the entire economic pyramid. Of course human beings are genetically programmed to be greedy and given the choice with all other barrier removed, the vast majority of people would want to be materialistic and wealthy. But are we as human beings genetically stuck on this path of avarice that has historically created a great divide between the rich and everyone else?

The notion of a heaven on earth, a Garden of Eden or Nirvana share common facets of freedom from suffering and struggle. If an ideal world is worth striving for because it is possible, then every child born should have the basic right to adequate:

1.	Food	2.	Shelter
3.	Education	4.	Medical care
5.	Love and affection	6.	Religious freedom
7.	Reasonable liberties	8.	Safety
9.	Protection from exploitation	10.	Freedom of association
11.	Pursuit of personal choices	12.	Employment
13.	Respect and dignity	14.	Freedom from fear

How could society insure these very basic entitlements are available to all within the context of the rule of law, capitalism and constitutionally guaranteed freedoms and rights?

1. Food to be based on nutritional standards, supplemented for the impoverished

2. Shelter based on free enterprise, govt./private/self-help partnership programs

3. Educational goals that provide personal choice, emphasize functional knowledge and skills development, good citizenship, ethics, and career goals

4. Medical care that is affordable, effective, and protects against catastrophes

5. Love and affection from effective parents, guardians, and communities

6. Peaceful religious practices of any type should be allowed; but not violence and hatred

7. Freedoms of speech, expression, assembly and press if not destructive

8. Protection from violent offenders; incarcerate predators and reprogram their brains

9. Non-exploitation through honest, transparent, and non-parasitic business practices

10. Freedom to choose association and exclusive clubs without government intervention

11. Pursuit of personal choices and happiness as long as not harming others

12. Sustainable employment with "living wages" and minimal taxation of low income workers

13. Respect, dignity, and civility; "do unto others as they should do to you."

14. Freedom from fear and intimidation by bullies, criminals, and authorities

The historical paradigm in human cultures and empires has always been the survival of the most ruthless, predatory, and brutal people. Human evolution has hopefully raised collective consciousness sufficiently to recognize that force, violence, and intimidation are barbaric and should be avoided as much as possible, but unfortunately bad habits die hard.

The framers of the U.S. Constitution shared a broad but common vision on the foundation of the rule of humanitarian process of governance that has endured for over 200 years, improving with successive generations of American idealism. We stand at another crossroad of generational change that could lead to the development of a common vision of social justice, economic security, ecological preservation, energy independence and global foreign policy. Who could speak against a nation and world that celebrates human achievement and social responsibility where all ships are uplifted by the rising tide? What would a practical and attainable future vision entail? Let's imagine how our nation and world can reasonably progress. Let's instill in our people positive visualizations of an attainable future where America takes the lead to better each citizen and resident as an example to the entire world.

Unfortunately, the war on terrorism has shown the world that the world is far from ideal and the forces of evil and destruction abound in almost every nation on earth, and usually takes on an anti-American form. The U.S. Congress and President are at odds and consequently are locked in partisan battles based upon philosophical and political differences. Barely recovering from the 2009 recession caused by the housing bubble burst, America once again is looking over the precipice of a potential economic melt down even though the Wall Street has regained all of its losses by election day 2012. No sooner was President Obama re-elected when die hard Republicans exploited CIA scandals to attack the administration, putting the President on the defensive and tossing out the first volley against cooperation and making bipartisanism again a fleeting rhetorical goal. Congress should make a list of all the issues that confront our great nation, then check off in four columns where they agree, disagree, that's open to compromise and what are the hard lines in the dirt. Then fix what they already agree on.

A practical solution to Congressional gridlock is relatively simple – remove the egotism and political posturing for the next election and do the business the people elected officials wisely accomplish on their behave. How? Let's look at how technology can remove the egos from the issues so solutions can be found instead if the status quo personal attacks and scandals that seem to preoccupy our elected leaders.

A secure access computer program will allow all lawmakers to state their beliefs and preferences and the degree of passion that they have for each issue. Legislative analysts will determine based upon sound impartial statistical, demographic and economic data what the impact of each proposed law will be on the federal budget and deficit. A legislation template will automatically complete all the typical legalese and identify the departments that will be assigned the tasks of implementation or enforcement without the creation of more bureaucracy. Each lawmaker will be able to review every proposed law and see where other elected officials fare on any particular issue.

For example, a legislator simply completes a checklist for every proposed bill, such as:

- Comprehensive immigration policy proposal: On a provisional scale of 1-10, with 10 indicating the highest level of agreement and 1 the greatest disagreement and 5 indicating unsure, complete the following legislative checklist for the above proposed legislation.
- Undocumented aliens shall be deported if arrested for commission of any crimes against persons or property or illegal behaviors as defined by federal statutes

- Undocumented aliens who serve in any branch of the U.S. armed forces, including the respective state National Guard or U.S. Coast Guard shall be granted a reprieve from deportation and will be permitted the opportunity to apply for permanent residency.

- Those undocumented aliens who become eligible for provisional permanent residency due to military service shall enable their immediate dependents (spouse and children only) to remain in the U.S. pending the approval of their application for permanent residency.

- Industry or government may sponsor certain foreign nationals for provisional permanent residency status if their highly technical or scientific skills are needed by corporations or any level of government where exhaustive searches for American citizens with commensurate skills are not fruitful to fill existing critical positions.

- In neither case shall undocumented aliens granted permanent citizenship be permitted to become citizens of the U.S. unless they first return to their native lands to file the appropriate applications for regular permanent residency and wait in line for their case reviews by the U.S. Immigration Service. However their provisional permanent residency status will remain in effect until such time as regular permanent status is granted, at which time existing laws pertaining to application to become U.S. citizens shall prevail.

Legislative analysts have determined that the fiscal impact of the above sections are likely to be as follows:

1) Deportation covered within existing departmental budget projections

2) There would be a likely 10% savings of deportation costs, however an increase to local and state adjudication and incarceration costs according to state and local statutes and priorities.

3) The administrative costs would be minimal and within existing budgets as the estimated number of individuals eligible under these sections is less than 20,000 per year. Tax revenues from the employment of provisional permanent residents should off set any administrative processing costs.

The employment impact of granting provisional permanent status to undocumented veterans would potentially decrease job opportunities for American citizens by less than 0.1%, and corporate sponsorship of highly skilled provisional status residents would have no impact on citizens if exhaustive searches do not disclose or attract qualified Americans.

Legislators would examine the proposed bill, including fiscal and bureaucratic budgetary impact and put their preliminary vote preferences. Taking the 100 Senators as an example, the non – binding pre-legislation vote on the proposed bill could be for each section of the bill. Consequently those sections of proposed bills that have a high probability of passage should move to the floor for discussion and vote. Those with little chance of passing should be removed from the bill.

This method reduces conflict as everyone's pre-legislation votes and scaling can be viewed by all legislators before presentation on the floor. Agreement is accentuated and discussion of polarized views that are not likely to pass are eliminated instead of resulting in lengthy partisan bickering and castigations that kills even the best parts of any proposed legislation.

What's the Main Reason Congress Can't Get Things Done?

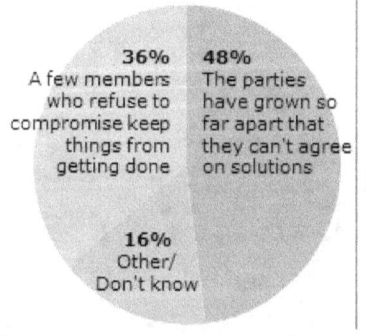

36%
A few members who refuse to compromise keep things from getting done

48%
The parties have grown so far apart that they can't agree on solutions

16%
Other/ Don't know

	Few members	Parties so far apart
Democrat	52	34
Independent	32	52
Republican	25	62

PEW RESEARCH CENTER Sept. 25-29, 2013.

Chapter 3 – America's Reality

America is fighting off attacks from both "supposed friends" and foes alike. The patriotic and uncorrupted officials in our government are working 24/7 to protect the United States from international and domestic conspirators who desire to see America fall to its knees, in order for them to gain power, prestige and wealth. Consequently there exist an evolving agenda to disrupt, manipulate and control the economy and government of the United States of America for the benefit of a various powerful domestic and foreign groups. Most of these schemes and plots have been reported sporadically by the national television news media and in more depth by political and news magazines. The strategies being employed can be deceptively disguised and hidden from discovery; however, they appear right under our noses in tactics such as:

1. Corrupt politicians who owe their allegiances to special interest groups who are funded or bribed by America's competitors, foes, foreign governments, criminal enterprises, and rouge despots.

2. Criminal organizations, their criminal activities and crime networks that possess high level connections to executives in the banking, investments, insurance and political networks. We need not look very far to discover a pattern of social entanglement between financiers and traffickers in the domestic and international drug trade, which generates funds for illegal arms trading that provide terrorists with their caches.

3.   Corrupt bureaucrats who have been enticed by slick, tricky, and dishonest investment brokers and bankers to squander public funds on ridiculous, speculative and highly risky investment scams. How can local and state government treasurers live lifestyles that exceed the means of their salaries? The Orange County fiasco with Merrill Lynch and the California budget deficit are "smoking guns" as records should prove our local governments and taxpayers have been swindled. How many bureaucrats and elitists have access to secret off-shore numbered accounts with funds from secret brides and kickbacks that enable them to evade taxes?

The Greeks were the greatest and most advanced democratic and technological civilization or their time. Yet, the great Greek civilization eventually fell, and history has clearly delineated the causes of its decline. Is America, the greatest and most advanced democratic and technological civilization of recent times vulnerable to similar patterns that led to the fall of the great Greek empire? Are there concerted secretive alliances that form an international conspiracy that is attempting to control strategic segments of American society, government, economy, education system, media, and laws?   There is ample evidence, based on public records and news reports, that points to conspiratorial networks who are working 24/7 to undermine, destabilize and manipulate the American system to their own advantage and benefit. Where are the hubs of this geo-political conspiracy? We need not look very far.

4.   The tentacles of these elite groups reach to America's greatest cities - Chicago, Las Vegas, New York City, Boston, New Jersey, Miami, Washington D.C., San Francisco, Houston, and Los Angeles. These networks of high financiers provide the funds for illegal activities, which they see as just another avenue to high and often illegal profits. These networks have access to criminal organizations that provide the foot soldiers and infrastructure required to move drugs, illegal arms, human trafficking other financial crimes and illegal activities. These same groups of financiers then use their banks and firms to launder money from illegally gotten gains from criminal organizations, as they collect their commissions for sanitizing the finances of the crime syndicates and terrorist networks.

5.   The players in this expansive clandestine network includes very legitimate names in banking, commodities and mercantile exchanges, investment banking, stock brokerages, corporate CEOs, CFOs and Board Chairs and Directors, accounting and auditing firms, politicians at all levels, corrupt local law enforcement officials, bureaucrats, foreign spies, military contractors and subcontractors, and special interest lobbyists (many who are actually foreign spies). Cooperating with this group of financiers and gatekeepers are the crime syndicates, drug cartels, and various terrorist groups, including Osama Bin Laden (now deceased) and Al Qaeda. These networks form an underground network of high finances that is hidden from the federal government, regulatory agencies, the Department of Treasury, the I.R.S., and F.B.I. administrators. The types of illegal investments and activities include:

a.   Money laundering, off shore tax havens, and secret bank accounts used to clean and hide "dirty money."

b.   Drug trafficking, financing, and corporate fronts.

c.   Illegal arms trade to states and terrorists.

d.   Corruption of key officials in our government, agencies, law enforcement, corporations and political parties.

e.   Stock market and commodities price manipulations, insider trading and other illegal trading practices, bribery, kickbacks, embezzlement, falsification of accounting records, tax evasion, and other financial crimes.

f.   Use of hedge funds and capital from wealthy individuals to invest in various schemes to short stocks and to attack monetary values, to crash stock markets and to cause hyper-inflation if it serves to turn a quick profit, even at the risk of collapsing the American economy.

g.   Multi-national corporations (MNCs) that do substantial business or receive investment or accounts consultation from members of these clandestine high finance networks can secretly provide logistical support for spies to access American technology at the point of production.

h. For example, if a foreign government wants to obtain secrets to America's Joint Strike Fighter, MNCs and their American subsidiaries can act to transfer technology from military contracts to the "go-between" spies, who then sell it or give it to our enemies and competitors.

In the past decade, it has been through this elaborate conspiracy network that Bin Laden became party to selling Afghan/Taliban heroin to Columbian and Mexican drug cartels through Mafia connections, whose money was then laundered by banks, investment brokerages and corporate executives who invested in drug deals. When Bin Laden's $500 million drug shipment was seized in April 2001, he needed to recoup his losses.

It was Bin Laden's intent to convert drug monies into arms and WMDs that included purchasing brief case nukes from the Chechens, which he then could have sleeper cells plant in various cities across the United States (this arguably had already been done by one of our supposed allies at the turn of the century). It was Bin Laden's plan to detonate all such implanted nukes by having one of his lieutenants call from a prepaid or stolen cell phone to trigger the WMDs. One of the "modus operendi" of Bin Laden was to execute well-planned multi-prong large attacks that could kill large numbers of innocent people, while driving a spike into the heart of the American economy. What's his group up to next? He managed to escape capture for a decade until President Obama acting on credible intel ordered his assassination. Our Homeland Security Department still has a monumental job ahead.

Al Qaeda is but one strategy to attempt to weaken Americans and the U.S. government, American culture, and way of life. The long-range goal of various anti-American conspirators is simple, and we are now witnessing the results of its insidious plot as society decays in all areas.

1.   Social decay by propagating disunity among Americans.

    a. Fuel racism by blaming whites for all of society's ills, to drive a wedge between minority races and the majority.

    b. Promote immorality and divisive cultural-ethnic-racial-sex conflicts by legalizing homosexual marriages, illegal immigration, pornography, affirmative action, late term abortion, and encouraging moral degeneration through mass media and television programming.

    c. Promote interracial conflict by creating ineffective and costly minority hand out programs that pits one race against another to the dismay of white tax payers.

    d. Create disrespect for authority and government by slowly outlawing basic freedoms, and creating too much red tape and large fines for too many minor infractions.

    e. Cause ethical and moral decay by outlawing reasonable corporal punishment of children for destructive conduct, where a reasonable degree of punishment by parents and teachers would otherwise keep certain students from future lives of crime. Instead, disrespectful children become rebellious teens who eventually spend most of their lives as adults in prison, becoming subjected to highly violent environments that far exceed the penalty of a loving spanking when it could have made a positive difference in their young lives.

    f. Suppress and ridicule good citizenship and patriotism, while promoting sex, violence, and greed as the "cool" and desirable lifestyle among our youth.

    g. Resist progressive changes to the education system, such as school vouchers. Mix all children into template classes, where disinterested and disruptive children ruin the learning environment for students who wish to learn. Penalize teachers by making them liable for false and frivolous accusations from various dysfunctional students.

2. Political decay by the media and universities that encourage distrust of government, particularly the federal government.

    a. Special interest groups and political lobbyists entice and corrupt government officials, politicians, and bureaucrats.

    b. Alienate citizens from governance by making them feel disinterested and hopeless to positively change policies.

When citizens no longer monitor government activities, there is greater latitude for corruptive influences to make significant inroads.

c.   Persuade corrupted legislators and agency chiefs to make policies that favor special interest groups, while punishing citizens, thereby transferring citizens' money to elites.

3.   Economic decay is evidenced by a strategy of wealth transfer from the working middle class to special interests elites.

a.   The U.S. A. is treated as just another consumer market for exploitation and wealth building by the elites, thus the ends justify the means, and patriotism is not a consideration.

b.   Swindle retirees of their life savings and pension plans through clever investment ruses and fraud. Enron, Arthur Andersen and Merrill Lynch corruption is only the tip of the iceberg. Law enforcement must identify and round up the corrupt executives from these conspiratorial networks to prevent them from corrupting every person, business, politician, and government official that they touch and bribe; otherwise, corruption will breed like cockroaches, and will become near impossible to exterminate.

c. Use technology to replace American workers, to maximize corporate profits and CEO compensation under the guise of fiscal necessity and competitive survival, instead of greed.

d. Outsource manufacturing and white collar high tech jobs to cheap labor markets, even if the consequence is harmful to the U.S. economy.

e. Concentrate control of strategic industries, raw materials, and consumer markets to MNCs whose executives have no loyalty to America, but only to wealth building.

f. Destabilize the U.S. dollar, by causing sudden massive monetary devaluation, then de-dollarize international trade when the monetary and trade imbalances makes the U.S. currency ripe for hedge fund speculation and attacks.

4. International relations decay by attempting to discredit, isolate and alienate the American President and our nation on the world stage.

a. Implement anti-American propaganda tactics through the news and mass media.

b. Use the elitist domestic and international news media to foment anti-American sentiments through biased news editing, reporting, and commentary represented as factual.

c. Foment violence, conflicts and insurgency to test American diplomatic and military response, and to stretch out America's resources abroad, thereby weakening American frontlines and borders.

d. Criticize U.S. response as being either too little too late, too heavy-handed and unilateralist, or too insensitive, or whatever slant is necessary to discredit America's good deeds abroad.

e. Foster anti-American sentiments to unify different political and religious camps by recognizing the U.S.A. as their common foe, by applying the "Your enemy's enemy is your friend" principle. This strategy is being used among Islamic states, anti-Semitic groups, and terrorist networks. A unified Europe, Sino-Russian rapprochement, and unified South America all present potential hot spots in fomenting future anti-American sentiments.

5. Military decay through compromise, spying, and overextension.

a. U.S. dependency on foreign manufacturers, suppliers, and raw materials needed for military hardware and systems.

b. Spies and moles are planted in sensitive government agencies, departments, and committees with oversight over intelligence, military technology, procurement, and operations.

c.   Government contracts and subcontracts that allow foreign corporations (thus governments) to monitor our military and government communication through service providers of email, phone, fax, computer hardware and software.

d.   Installation of "back door" chips or spy software in military and government computer networks and equipment, such as computers, planes, trucks, offices, and ships to enable spying by foreign governments.

e.   Integration of "override" chips or software programs into military weapons and communications systems to permit partial or complete take over, sabotage, or destruction of vulnerable military systems, such as virtual battlefield and the Joint Strike Fighter.

f.   Install spy technology into sensitive American facilities, buildings, vehicles, and offices through construction, art work, furniture, equipment, housekeeping and security.

With the advent of this new millennium, we entered into a new global paradigm, where interrelationships between bankers and stockbrokers become intermingled with the mutual monetary goals of drug cartels, illegal arms merchants, enemy states, corrupt politicians, criminal syndicates, and international terrorists. The flow of drugs and weapons is often financed by diverting legitimate funds, with illegal profits washed clean through money-laundering networks abetted by domestic and international banks. It has become difficult to track down the financiers of terrorism only because on the surface they appear to be legitimate individuals, usually above suspicion, but occupying high perches from which great financial benefits are derived.

The majority of Americans support our government's effort to protect our homeland from attacks, and even though we suspect no system is perfect, there may yet be times terrorists will be somewhat successful in causing wanton death, destruction, and mayhem. President George W. Bush is the first American president to place our nation on a "proactive" footing - a political stance similar to the Truman Doctrine to contain the spread of communism, where rather than to wait to be attacked by our enemies first then react after the fact, America reserves the right to strike if facts on the ground clearly indicate the security of the United States is at dire risk. The old adage, "an ounce of prevention is worth a pound of cure" is still very appropriate in our new post-modern high tech era, in our nation's concerted effort to defeat our true enemies (terrorists states who support terrorists). However, as long as the majority of the world's people remain poor and destitute, they are likely to become the fodder and foot soldiers for madmen and terrorists. Armed with new cell phone technology, grass root insurrection may be a tweet away.

Our homeland and military are exposed to many areas of vulnerability, and the problems that have been revealed amount to just the "tip of the iceberg." Mega-greed knows no loyalty to nation, culture, ideals, or people. Greedy people are hypocrites, serpents, and a brood of vipers. To those who worship money, the ends justify the means, and they are fully capable of employing any means necessary to achieve their greedy financial goals. Terrorism, drug dealing, illegal arms trade, mega-corporate mergers, political corruption and investment scams are just the tools that are employed to derive their ill gotten wealth. A house divided can not stand long, consequently as the multi-pronged attacks against fundamental American institutions continue to go unabated, our enemies can greatly weaken America by influencing or controlling key U.S. communication and administrative hubs that could fatally compromise our military, political, economic, social, and international relations institutions and personnel. Our enemies' common agenda is to bring America down.

In this life, there are primarily ten ways to accumulate great wealth through:

- Inheritance from the wealth of others now deceased
- Entrepreneurial ventures such as small businesses to fortune 500
- Creativity, talents and invention such as new technologies
- Land ownership and development
- Discovery and exploitation of natural resources such as oil and minerals
- High end of professional services such as top attorneys and accountants
- Middleman dealings such as stock brokers
- Investments, gambling and financial manipulations
- Criminal activities
- nepotistic military juntas.

The first six ways to wealth are primarily above board, transparent and honest. The next two are nebulous and subject to risky decisions that primarily move money around using various contractual means. The final two are predatory and often deadly.

The problem is too much of our national and global economy is greased by the actions of the latter four ways to wealth building and there isn't much interest to change anything soon.

Globalization and the rapid rise of MNCs, elitist CEOs and oligarchs signal the rapid demise of ethics, morality, umanitarianism and patriotism. We need not look too far to the event horizon to see our potential futures destroyed by international carpetbaggers and terrorists. We must win the war on the secret financiers of global terrorism soon, otherwise it will be too little, too late. A concerted attack on the international monetary system through various financial or cyber strategies could doom the world to worse case scenarios.

Our nation and the world sits atop a huge financial bubble where most of the world's wealth is created from thin air. Governments print fiat monies that are loaned to bankers at preferred rates not available to the populace. The banks who exert great control over the central banks of their respective nations then attempt to make outrageous CEO profits by placing heavy bets on the securities market, often betting and shorting the sovereign debt of entire nations such as Greece, Iceland, Spain and so on. When these bankers profit by disrupting the normal cash flow of nations they stand to benefit on the international monetary exchange if they bet right and bet big. The solution to almost all of these financial problems created by schemes and manipulation is simply to require complete transparency through the entire process of executing financial instruments. If nothing can be hidden, then it is honest. Too many of the world's cultures have become westernized where the "s" in the word stands for secrecy. Were more people, elected officials and governments to live and function in the light of transparency, instead of hiding under the cloak of secrecy, then communications and therefore solutions would be more forthcoming.

But law makers and CEOs would claim that transparency would expose and destroy necessary military and industrial secrets. Naturally those secrets would remain hidden, but the vast majority of secrets should in fact be public knowledge to prevent the corruptive temptation of operating in the shadows. At the same time, what if every nation on earth realized there is a doomsday bomb that can explode the entire earth from below the mantle? Would that cause a proliferation in stealing doomsday technology and cause a new doomsday arms race? If so, then perhaps mankind is a lot stupider than they often seem and in the final analysis humans as a species is either driven by their genetic fate to progress or to become extinct. It would be my bet that the vast majority of people and leaders in the world don't want to lose what they already have and their future opportunities to amass greater wealth, property, material things and power and thus transparency might cause them to have greater insights and responsibilities for their actions and those of their neighbors and nations.

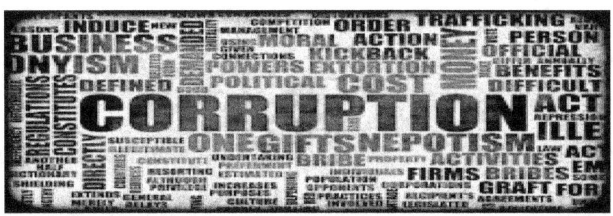

Chapter 4 – Americas Future

Our domestic economy is comprised in excess of 80 percent by service sector jobs, hitch indicates it is primarily based on people relying on others to do what they lack the adequate skills, time, or desire to achieve. It's an economy based upon an abundance of ignorance, laziness, and conveniences. Common sense would suggest that ignorance, laziness and convenience are not precursors of a competitive economic system in a global paradigm, as compared to economics based upon knowledge, expertise, effort, and perseverance.

The infrastructure and relationships within the American economy may portend an inherent weakness toward eventual and sudden collapse, as artificial stock, employment, and monetary value bubbles burst. Critics would argue that the American economy is the strongest that the modern world has ever seen, with GDP over $13 trillion annually. However, several recent events indicate the U.S. economy is subject to severe fluctuations, such as those which almost bankrupted several economic sectors after the "911" terrorist attacks, in addition to the "dot-com" collapse only a year earlier and more recently the housing bubble bust and hyperinflation oil prices.

Let's examine a plausible scenario based upon current economic and geo-political trends. By the year 2010, with Germany, France, and all European nations will share a common monetary system and Great Britain (UK), pressured by economic necessity, would eventually join the E.U. China's burgeoning growth, coupled with Japan's capitalization has the potential to become a regional partnership powerhouse in Asia, each holding vast sums of American dollars, together producing the majority of products consumed by Americans.

Americans may dread the day when a united EU-UK, coupled with a united Asia, with Russia as a bi-lateral trading partner of both, cooperate to provide economic pressure against the United States. Juxtaposed against this dire economic backdrop could be unrelenting conflict in the Middle-East, as Arabs continue to resist Israeli power and presence in former Arab lands. The consequences of heightened Jewish economic power and Israeli military power could bring about another oil crisis, as Arab states retaliate against supporters of the Jewish state – in particular the United States, Israel's protector. Already, the U.S. relies almost entirely on foreign manufacturers to produce dozens of strategic components required by its most advanced weapons systems. Americans are becoming increasingly dependent on less expensive imports to offset a drop in real purchasing power, as U.S. corporations continue to build factories and export American jobs overseas or south of the border to cheap labor markets.

The internal economy, upon which U.S. GDP (gross domestic product) data accrues Is comprised by measuring the spending of American consumers, government, investors, and net exports. Carving up the $17.5 trillion annual U.S. GDP indicates that government spending (federal, state, local, etc.) accounts for over $5 trillion, consumerism for another $5 trillion, and investments of about $5 trillion annually (not including the $trillion budget deficit from two wars against terrorism) . A projected federal deficit of $1 trillion (not to mention states, such as California's $17 billion budget deficit), and a deepening trade deficit exceeding $500 billion annually suggest that our domestic economic bubble is comprised to a great extent on illusory spending. The U.S. national debt now exceeds $18 TRILLION, which has now surpassed the nation's $17.5 trillion GDP – further indebting future generations to indentured servitude.

According to wikipedia.com, "On June 30, 2014, debt held by the public was approximately $12.6 trillion or about 74% of Q1 2014 GDP. Intragovernmental holdings stood at $5.1 trillion (30%), giving a combined total public debt of $17.6 trillion or about 104% of Q1 2014 GDP. As of January 2013, $5 trillion or approximately 47% of the debt held by the public was owned by foreign investors, the largest of which were the People's Republic of China and Japan at just over $1.1 trillion each."

What might happen to the U.S. economy were certain foreign interests to make sudden enormous liquidation of U.S. currency, stocks, bonds, and real estate investments? A rapid spiraling drop in consumer confidence would surely follow such wholesale destructive market movements. In 1997, the manipulation of billions of dollars of hedge funds by a single man greatly contributed to the near collapse of the Asian monetary exchange market, contributing to severe devaluation of the domestic currencies in Indonesia, Malaysia, Korea, and other SE Asian countries. Could a similar scenario happen right here in the United States of America? A large coordinated attack against the U.S. dollar could cripple the American economy, and drive the U.S. into a severe economic depression, with only the treat of worldwide thermonuclear war as a subsequent and real deterrent against foreign economic domination or invasion.

The fundamental question remains; "Does the U.S. have the capacity to survive independently of international trade, were our current trading partners to become our trading competitors or enemies instead?" What could happen if foreign governments such as Saudi Arabia and other oil producing nations were to conspire to "de-dollarize" their oil exports, such that U.S. dollars would no longer be accepted as payment for crude oil? Would the U.S. be forced to drain our precious oil reserves, and then trade our limited gold and transfer military hardware and technology in barter for oil? Certainly, under such circumstances, the U.S. economy would immediately go into shock, with run-away inflation that will create an out-of-control cycle of massive job loss, plummeting stock market values, widespread personal and business bankruptcies, and destruction of capital and capital assets.

Under such a scenario, the U.S. economy would experience a paralysis not seen since the Great Depression of the 1930's, and would call for Uncle Sam to start another round of FDR-style public employment programs to save the economy. But where would the federal government find tax dollars to spend? States and local governments would become bankrupt, and there would be insufficient taxes collected from the shrinking employed population to fund any ambitious government-backed employment program. A precursor of America's future economic problems may be experienced by California (arguably the sixth largest economy in the world), as its bonds were valued just above "junk" by bond rating companies less than 4 years ago. Is it conceivable that U.S. government bonds could also become "junk" someday? Simply printing more money to pay off existing bonds and debts held by foreign investors would not clear the ledger, without causing the complete collapse and rejection of the dollar as a medium of international trade.

Were such global conspiracies among our potential competitors and foes to materialize, what could the U.S. government do to survive, while leading Americans back into solvency? Already, multi-national corporations approach the world as one global marketplace, without any loyalty to nation, creed, or politics. Profit making and profit taking is all that drives the global economy as capitalism without any morals or consideration of future perils. America's largest corporations have taken on the appearance of money-making vehicles to return exorbitant CEO compensation packages, to the detriment of both stockholders and employees.

Corporate profits are often not reinvested back into the domestic economy in the form of stockholder dividends, new hiring, and investment in buildings and equipment. Instead, profits are taken out of the U.S., and hidden in offshore tax-free havens, or invested overseas in nations with low standards of living with abundant cheap labor. How do irresponsible corporate actions contribute to strengthening the American economy? It doesn't, and instead places America in potential economic peril.

PROTECTING AMERICA FROM RUINATION

How can our government protect us against such worse-case scenarios? The recent federal efforts to stimulate the economy has had limited and sporadic success. Lowering the federal discount rate certainly has benefited banks and financial institutions, encouraged home purchasing and the housing inflation bubble, loan refinancing, and had somewhat stimulated car purchasing, but it has not resulted in more jobs that would provide more spendable income for average Americans. The lower cost of borrowing money is not producing real gains because corporations and wealthy individuals are not reinvesting the surplus capital into the domestic economy, and continue to lay off thousands of workers as part of corporate strategy to enhance CEOs' stock options. The tax cut, while well-intentioned to provide more discretionary dollars to consumers is easily absorbed by runaway credit card debts and increased housing costs. The added $300-$600 tax break for most wage earners doesn't cover the added cost of consumer debt, as the tax cut is primarily transference of money from wage earners to creditors, lenders, oil companies and landlords. The most important issue apparently being missed by Washington insiders is the continued loss of consumer confidence that results from the fear of job loss. As more workers lose confidence in the longevity of their jobs, they tend to abstain from making large purchases and try to hang on to the little savings that they have for that stormy period that seems to linger on the horizon.

It's become urgent for the U.S. to develop economic targets that can be realistically achieved by the U.S. economy against the larger backdrop of global competition. What economic policies could effectively turn around a sluggish economy while protecting its foundation against future peril and attacks? Firstly, we must develop a national vision of our economic future, set goals, and put into place national strategies to grow the economy while protecting against inflation, deflation, high unemployment, wild stock market speculation, higher budget deficit spending, and the transference of wealth to international conglomerates and speculators who have no qualms about robbing the life out of America for short-term gains.

We must not rely solely on tax cuts and lower interest rates to stimulate the economy because middle class consumers benefit relatively slightly, while the wealthy and corporate elites have not shown a desire to reinvest excess profits back into their commercial enterprises in America. Without placing substantial discretionary funds into the pockets of wage earners, coupled with increasing belief that the public will have jobs, consumers will hesitate to spend. Without added spending, economic activity remains sluggish and any systemic shock or external attacks against the economy would likely cause a slide into a long lasting recession, and possible economic depression. The engine that drives economic stability and the GDP is economic activity based on consumer confidence. When the public has confidence, the society and nation prospers.

America must become more independent of foreign trade to obtain manufactured goods. The U.S. must gain direct benefits from their occupation of Iraqi oilfields to stabilize oil prices. Agricultural products should be supported as a major source to balance our trade deficit, and to act as an anchor to ensure that our trading partners will continue to accept the U.S. dollar as payment for their imported goods. High tech industries, defense, biotechnologies, pharmaceuticals, and scientific research must be supported and freed from excessive red tape. These fields provide the foundation for future economic growth, protection against foreign competitors, and a safety margin against terrorism and conspiracies against the American economy, while improving the quality of life for current and future generations of Americans.

Immigration must be controlled, and all illegal foreign nationals must be identified, rounded up, and deported, starting with criminals - which will decrease the demand for expensive and extensive infrastructure services for over 10 million illegal immigrants, thus saving vast amounts spent on public education, public housing, healthcare, social services, law enforcement, and incarceration of illegal immigrants - that would result in restoring local and state governments to solvency. Displaced public sector workers would be forced to find jobs in the private sector or to become more entrepreneurial. A legal documented workers program would allow specific numbers of foreign nationals to work no more than 3 consecutive years in the U.S. in occupations begging for workers before having to return to their homeland for at least one year.

These foreign guest workers would have to pay their fair share of taxes, and there would be no promise of amnesty, permanent residency or citizenship. In this way, they can become legal and not have to worry about being rounded up or breaking up their families, or becoming victims of predators who exploit the fear of immigrants to interact with law enforcement.

The public education system must be revamped and redesigned to provide the highly educated and trained professionals that are required by high tech, defense and scientific industries. We can no longer accept a broken public school system that produces the lowest performers among western nations. As long as our public school system continues to turn out students who are basically ignorant, lazy, and seekers of conveniences, we will continue to be trapped in an economy that depends on the purchase of services to compensate for stupidity.

It is essential for mass media to take a more responsible path that contributes to improving society, rather than to encourage and exploit scandals, human conflict, and baser escapist drives for the sake of advertising dollars and commercial profits. Television, movies, and computer games have become the media of destruction, where fun is equated to massive destruction, killing, profanity, and disregard for moral and responsible conduct. Our youth are being programmed into destroyers, who are able to delve inordinate hours in fantasy instead of spending time creating worthwhile things, pursuing constructive activities, or supporting their communities. This continuing trend is not healthy for a civilization that is becoming ever less civilized. Without a civil and educated citizenry who will be capable of maintaining a complex high tech economy of the future, we may be doomed to suffer the consequences of our present failures. Our nation flounders as the students drop out in record numbers, primarily because we do not have a national vision.

We need to minimize the adversarial relationships within our government. Too much political conflict results from factions who spend inordinate time, energy, and expense to sabotage their competitors' legislative and political agendas. The drive for power, and to win at all cost invariable leads to a destructive course where personality innuendoes and not public issues become the fodder of the day. The supposed healthy public discourse rarely materializes, and instead is replaced by tidbits of media sound bites designed for the comprehension and consumption of fourth graders. Democracy becomes muffled by rumors, misstatements, and media biases. There's a time for competition (hopefully without dirty tricks, slander, and scandals), but more often, there's more reason to invest time on finding cooperative common grounds for solving the people's problems.

The people want answers and solutions, much more than the political squabbling and infighting that seem to typify our government leaders. Give the people what they want, a stable and prosperous economy based upon a capitalist market system that is not corrupted by excessive greed, fraud and dishonesty. Our genius federal forefathers designed a political and economic system of the people, for the people, and by the people. Let's ensure that proper actions are taken to safeguard this great nation, America, against the economic perils of the present and future.

THE CURRENT ECONOMIC MODEL IS FLAWED

The current economic paradigm is built upon certain suppositions that include:

- Money is the purchase of debt, which has value
- Debt is the promise of future value in exchange for money
- Consumer confidence supports the value of debt in exchange for materialism
- The monetary system is an accounting system that tracks and manages debt
- Foreign exchange is an arbitrary assignment of value by global financial gatekeepers
- The creation of legitimate debt creates economic value
- The elites have ways to modify the numbers and its effect on changing debt value
- Gatekeepers can cheat for personal benefit and gain
- Debt is used as a method of global development
- Using debt as usury has a long term detrimental effect
- Alternative monetary systems are in place that act to increase the level of debt such as electronic credit/debits, promissory notes, public and private bonds

The reality is the accumulation of money acts to exploit the masses of laborers and consumers as money has become an intermediary debt transference device with a promise of future value that can not be assured. To the owners of debt, the masses become an asset – but to the debtors, debt is the ball and chain that slows down their ability to otherwise succeed. Consequently, true value in a technologically dependent world requires investing in energy sources that are not slaves to oil because money would become worthless in any amounts when the oil supplies run out within a couple of generations. The true source of the growth and stability of long term wealth is the health of human resources that perform the roles of both producer and consumer, allowing the ownership stakeholders to increase personal wealth.

WINNING IN IRAQ WILL HELP AMERICA TO GET OUT OF DEBT
      (written circa 2008)

Americans want to help our brave troops to win the war in Iraq so less American lives will be lost. The next elected President must complete the execution of President Bush's Iraq policy so Americans can feel success and our nation won't become divided as during the latter days of the Vietnam War. Let's make sure this time around American blood will have been shed for a glorious purpose and outcome. After 5 years of the Iraq War, the U.S. Treasury has hemorrhaged almost a trillion dollars – all deficit spending. When will the spilling of American blood result in tangible results that benefit Americans, our economy and our international image?

So, how do we win in Iraq? We've been primarily fighting a low-tech block by block war, and if history has demonstrated anything, it is the side with the better technology who is capable of killing a substantially higher ratio of enemy to friendly who will win every time. The kill ratio in Iraq is highest when IEDs and suicide bombers kill more soldiers, policemen and innocents than any predator missile. Fighting a low-tech block by block war gives insurgents, jihadists, and al Qaeda more even odds – waiting for our voters to lose interest and our politicians to de-fund the war effort as the precursor to a complete pull out of American troops. Pulling out simply to save our butts would be seen as a dismal failure and America will again be accused of being a paper tiger.

We need a new Iraq strategy – more dedicated surveillance satellites to monitor all cell phone traffic with computer software screening of key words, floating balloon video surveillance of key problem areas, development of software to monitor congregation of people movement utilizing advance motion detection sensors and software matrix, improved monitoring of Islamic websites and email with computer tracing to source. As we all realize, it's particularly difficult to recruit native speaking Arabs whose accent would not foil their roles as CIA agents…and there's always the possibility of dual loyalties. Consequently, we must perfect robotic voice to speak fluent Arabic and the languages of our enemies and potential foes. As much communication between terrorist cells also utilize the Internet, steps must be taken to intercept, interpret and interdict such communications utilizing sophisticated instantaneous language translation software.

The goal of creating a singular democratic Iraq that is friendly to America is essential for ensuring our future access to oil and strategic positioning in the Middle-East. However, in order to minimize insurgency and to prevent a potential civil war, the new Iraqi government should designate a "Sunni province" where the security of Sunnis would be guaranteed (first by the joint US-coalition-Shia military forces, until national Iraqi police forces can stand up by themselves insure against Shia on Sunni retaliation). All Sunnis who desire a guarantee of peaceful coexistence would be encouraged to migrate to the secured Sunni green zone, a domestic self-governing subordinate province in the Iraq nation similar to the jurisdiction of statehood in a democratic republic form of government such as the US.

Sunnis who choose not to migrate to the Sunni province must register with the central Iraqi government, get fingerprinted and issued bio-metric photo I.D. cards which they must carry at all times, subject to arrest for non-compliance. U.S. and Iraqi troops will carry I.D. card readers that are linked to the master I.D. data base computer at Central Command. Anyone suspected of involvement with insurgency will be forced to accept a micro chip tracking implant that can be monitored by satellite to determine the location of any congregation of terrorists & insurgents. In which case, a well placed guided missile from a Predator drone would suffice.

The Kurds will be given adequate training and armament to protect themselves against Sunni or Iranian incursions, and the Shites will be responsible to stabilize Shia urban areas. Kurds and coalition forces will concentrate on interception and interdiction of foreign fighters who attempt border crossings to link with Sunni insurgents and al Qaeda fighters. Coalition forces to be redeployed as battalion sized rapid strike cavalry forces to respond to any substantial incursions of Sunni fighters outside of the Sunni province. Incentives will be given to Sunnis to stay within their own green zone, such as limited self-rule and increased economic aid in exchange for gradual disarmament. In the event Sunnis take the path to consolidate armaments instead of pursuing peace, coalition forces will be able to utilize advanced weapons systems to destroy their forces in mass, without street-to-street fighting, once the Sunni Province is determined to be a state.

The strategy is to isolate the Sunnis, by segregating them from the Shites, with coalition forces as the buffer initially, to be replaced by national Iraqi forces once they are capable. Subsequently, US-coalition resources can concentrate on killing foreign jihadists and al Qaeda fighters and containing Sunni excursions from their designated province. Coalition focus would not be spread out as in the current campaign – but instead would concentrate on problem areas, leaving less challenging maintenance and policing to the central Iraqi government.

The other side of the peace equation is to decrease the influence of Iranian Shia mullahs on Iraqi Shites. Shite on Sunni violence must also be brought under control with similar measures used to disarm and stabilize the Sunni green zone. Shite green zones must be developed where there is factional self-rule for domestic issues. Shites who leave their green zones without proper identification can be detained and they would be required to possess bio-metric I.D. cards or be computer chipped as with Sunnis who desire to operate outside of their green zone. There must be a much higher deployment of spy satellites over Iran to permit the U.S. to monitor Iran's nuclear ambitions, with intelligence sharing with Israel who will have no qualms to send military strikes to destroy any nuclear weapons ambition Iran is working to achieve. Should the Central Iraqi government fail to bring a free democratic secular government to Iraq, the alternative of creating a tripartite with 3 separate independent governments should be explored and probably implemented.

Threats to America and the free world are not limited to Iraq or even the Middle East. Other world arenas with potential problems for America include:

- Communism in So. America – We must keep an eye on the players through back door dialog and greater human intelligence.
- Zionism – We must take the course of gradual disengagement as Israel becomes safer and more able to protect herself from Arab enemies such as Iran and Syria. America should reduce its level of overt support and instead operate on unofficial levels, least we become pulled into all of Israel's problems.

- Islamic extremism – The official recognition of the importance of religious freedom for groups who emphasize doctrines and passages from the Koran that support peaceful relations should be pursued. Public denunciation of anti-western Islamic belief should be downplayed, but pressure should be placed on Arab leaders to keep the extremist madras and terrorists training camps in check. Increasing the unofficial support of moderate, peaceful and rational Islamic sects in exchange for their pledge not to preach anti-US, anti-Israel, and anti-western civilization dogma is essential for deterring yet another generation of haters whose life purposes becomes the destruction of the west through terrorism.
- Christian fundamentalism – Official government policies should not pander to Evangelical or ultra conservatives whose intolerance only tends to drive wedges between the general citizenry and non-believers. Emphasize religious tolerance, charity, and forgiveness.

WORLD CONFLICT ARISES FROM HUMAN PROPENSITIES

The world's peoples are divided, fragmented and segmented according to too many "isms" that have caused a schism in acknowledging that all humans share a common lineage – whether beliefs are founded in Judeo-Christian traditions, Islamic beliefs, Eastern religions or philosophies, Native American spiritualism, African indigenous customs, or in scientific theory and facts. No major framework of thought support the notion that all people are not from the same "family of man" – though we now know that women are the progenitors, without which men could not exist.

Yet with the abundance of knowledge and facts supporting the unified development, creation, or evolution of human beings, people still choose to divide themselves into separate camps based upon external and superficial differences to institutionalize "isms" such as elitism, classicism, racism, sexism, ageism, and legalism. These artificially enforced "isms" have the net effect of creating a world characterized by poverty, oligarchs, MNCs, political corruption, labor exploitation, bureaucratic corruption, greed and repetitive widespread warfare and genocide.

What stands in the way of a sensible and ecological path of development? The elites can still have their way and become wealthier without having to sacrifice the world's ecological health. Unfortunately, genetically ingrained human propensities create obstacles to developing a more civilized world and the universal adoption of a socially responsible mindset that is tolerant of human differences, respectful of the biosphere and its life forms, and accepting the responsibility to be stewards of humanity's future generations.

What genetic traits have kept humans primarily the same emotional creatures from the beginning of humanity? Ask a thousand people if they feel they are basically good people who care about others, and the vast majority, perhaps as high as 95% will believe in their own goodness, albeit admit they are far from perfection. The reality is homo sapiens remain primal and animalistic, even though technology appears to have given mankind an external makeover. The following inherited instincts continue to prevail generation after generation from the beginning of the human race and early civilizations:

- Hunting instinct
- Predatory instinct
- Gathering – hoarding – greed instinct
- Destructive instinct
- Parasitic instinct
- Exploitation instinct
- Control compulsion
- Sexual urge
- Power urge
- Physical stimulation urge
- Emotional insecurities propensity
- Criminality

What positive instincts serve to demonstrate the better side of humanity?

- Planting – building instinct
- Mental stimulation urge
- Spiritual balance need
- Art – music
- Entertainment
- Discovery
- Exploration
- Scientific knowledge
- Invention
- Physical work and recreation
- Humanitarianism
- Interdependency – need for family and belonging

Why does the majority of our world's population continue to be imprisoned by conflict, disease, starvation, poverty and misery? What are worthwhile pursuits that could correct the injustices and resource imbalances that are caused by institutionalized greed, corporate and political corruption, elitism, and prejudice? What comprehensive vision must be universally recognized in order for international policy makers to cooperate on joint ventures that can save our world from our worsening development and population pressures? Will things ever change for the better? Following are suggestions for tangible actions that should be taken to better our nation, America and the world to improve our chances of progress and survival into the next century.

A VISION OF SUSTAINABLE NATIONAL AND GLOBAL IMPROVEMENT

1.   Medical Research and Treatment
     a.   Pharmaceutical greed must be regulated to prevent exorbitant pricing for drugs that cost a pittance to manufacture, even after the inflated cost of development are factored In.

Unethical conflicts of interest exist among many FDA scientists and regulators who often share beds with the pharmaceutical giants and are "paid off" with lucrative consulting fees. No wonder "bad research" is sometimes permitted, where "safety and efficacy" issues are skirted to permit accelerated drug approval based upon flawed human trials. The Merck drug, Vioxx, is thought to contribute to over 150,000 heart attacks, strokes and other serious life threatening illnesses. Which panel of FDA reviewers permitted this drug to market? Were any of them also on the payroll of Merck? Meanwhile, the American public, particularly the drug-dependent elderly, is being gouged by greedy corporate CEOs who line their deep dirty pockets with legal "drug money", often causing retired, sick, and dying old people to decide between eating or the cost of medication.

Since the current FDA refuses to protect the American public against fraudulent claims and price gouging, then we need to impanel new public servants who have consciences and know the difference between right and wrong. The lives of America's elderly, sick and poor depend on a safe, efficacious, and responsibly priced drug policy that is enforced by bureaucrats and scientists who value the public good over kick back schemes and greed.

b.   Stem cell research using non-fetal sources must be pushed due to its great potential to permit individuals' own bodies to repair itself. Stem cell research is showing great potential in Asia, where many instances of recovery from permanently inoperable spinal cord injuries are now a reality from simple injections of stem cells. Asians, being primarily of non-Christian religions, do not view the use of fetal stem cells from placental material in the same way westerners view it. Asians do not see the harvesting of embryonic stem cells as destruction of human souls, which would not makes sense because with each month, billions of unfertilized human embryos are flushed down the world's toilets at the end of women's menstrual cycles. Why waste good embryos that can cure diseases, repair badly wrecked bodies, and possibly open the door to real cures for cancer, AIDS, and other debilitating and life threatening diseases? No doubt the pharmaceutical giants are the silent hands in urging conservative Christian leaders and politicians to protest and block stem cell research to protect their turf and profit making, which are greatly threatened by any stem cell successes. Who would need synthetic drugs anyway once stem cell is able to repair severe damage to internal organs, nerves, muscles, cells, and even brain tissue? Let's all remain ignorant and let countless millions of people suffer and die so greedy pharmaceutical CEOs can continue to profit in the game of life versus death.

  c. Genetic engineering modifications that will rid the human genome of diseased caused by mutations, viruses, and heredity are essential to reducing human suffering and the high cost of health care. Genetic engineering has the potential to literally restructure humanity to eliminate genetic defects, while improving the human genome. Imagine human beings who remain healthy, youthful, and vibrant late into their lives, perhaps extending average human lifespan to 150! Genetic engineering is thought to reintroduce the controversial racist preferences and claims of racial superiority spawned by the eugenics craze of the previous generation. In fact, were genetic engineering to be objectively used, every human being, regardless of race could become the best human being possible. With the possibility of so many people of all races and ethnicities walking the earth with 2 to 3 times their current potential, the old notions of racism, sexism, disability, ageism, and other "isms" would inevitably be replaced by a sense of universal egalitarianism, tolerance, and respect for individual differences.

  d. HMO greed has driven up the price of health care far surpassing the rationale for its initial creation – to lower the price of healthcare by keeping physician and hospital rates lower. The fact is, doctors and hospitals struggle to keep their offices open because they have essentially become employees of HMO's whose drive for profits does not pass on any lower rates to patients but instead serves to deny all but a modicum level of health care to people who possess medical insurance. HMO's must be kept in check from driving up the cost of health care. HMO greed has drastically driven up the cost of healthcare and reduced the quality of medical treatment that would otherwise be available to most Americans, particularly the elderly, "working poor", and the impoverished who are least able to afford healthcare. It isn't logical that the addition of another level of middlemen between the care giver and the patient could result in savings and a more affordable healthcare delivery system. If the average American could afford $2,000 annually for medical treatment, and the HMOs charge subscribers $1,500 annually for insurance premiums, $500 per person for annual deductibles, and another $500 for annual co-pays for visits and medicines, how's that helping to deliver more affordable healthcare services to patients?

Meanwhile HMO clerks and accountants routinely deny its members needed medical care because it constitutes added expenses against the profits of their CEOs. Where are the government regulatory agencies when you really need them to fix this broken healthcare system? What politicians are routinely being wined and dined by HMO lobbyists, who then vote on regulations and laws that benefit HMOs at the expense of tax paying Americans? Let's look at the voting records of our so-called government representatives to determine the conflict of interests.

e.   Equal access to services has been the recent health care debate. The insurance lobby has fought any plan that does not insure their profits or threaten to increase their outlay for benefits. Equal access to services is not possible in our greed driven capitalistic system that has no social conscience and is predicated on the profit motive to charge the highest amount that the market will bear. People's health needs, adequate and proper medical treatment, and saving lives becomes secondary to the "de facto" class system that is based upon one's ability to access affordable and decent health care. As the population ages and more people fall out of the middle class to fill the ranks of the working poor, society is faced with solving the basic philosophical hypocrisy, which claims life to be priceless. Certainly there is a price on life. If one can afford reputable healthcare insurance, their chances of living a life with minimal suffering greatly increases over that experienced by those who have little or no access to affordable healthcare, because healthcare has become unaffordable for one-third of all Americans. Where's the justice? Does a wealthy person have a greater right to life than a poor person, who may work equally as hard or even harder for a living? Statistics clearly show good health and longevity are dependent upon individual's economic health, class and race more than personal habits. Let's reform HMOs to follow the model of non-profit organizations such as Kaiser-Permanente, who builds hospitals, hire competent doctors and nurses, and provide its members with the highest quality of care that money can buy. Let's close down the for-profit greed-centered HMOs, which have driven up the price of healthcare beyond affordability for a large segment of Americans. That's in America's national interest.

2. Environmental Protection

a. Atmospheric pollution knows no boundaries. Acid rain falls across the Canadian-US borders from American industries. The jet stream takes chemical pollutants downwind across continents and particulate pollution from combustion engines eventually fall back on plants, soil, water, animals, roadways, and buildings, which are washed into the oceans and lakes with the next downpour. Ozone depletion from cow manure methane, vehicle AC Freon, and other industrial emissions may become irreversible if global development and pollution increases and remains unchecked. Any series of large volcanic explosions or nuclear warfare will be felt on a global basis, because we are all breathing the same air that has been recycled from the time of the great dinosaurs. Our atmosphere i a closed system, and we all breath health-threatening contaminants when we don't take effective measures to protect our life sustaining air supply.

b. Rivers, lakes and oceans are ecosystems that provide not only the potable water we need to remain alive, but is the environment for countless species of fish, plants, microorganism, and other forms of living things. When we pollute our water supply through industrial, agricultural, residential, and recreational wastes, we contaminate both our drinking water and the life that lives in the liquid dimension. The popularity of filtered and bottled water attests to the fact that people are often afraid to drink tap water due to its impurities.

c. Landfills are not only becoming dangers to our subterranean fresh water tables where many cities draw their drinking water, but they remain another increasing source of methane, which if not recycled is released into the atmosphere. Landfills become the resting place for unknown types and quantities of toxic materials, from mercury to oil and medical radioactive wastes that illegally find its way into trash bins. Landfills are rapidly becoming cheap land for the construction of residential subdivisions, city parks and golf courses, and where there's money to be made, bureaucrats will usually find justification to bend or ignore health and safety laws in favor of development and tax collection. Some day, residential tracts or children's playground which are built upon reclaimed landfills may spontaneously burst into flames from the methane buildup, or there will be great increases in the number of unusual childhood cancer cases and the public uproar will result in lawyers making more money before homes are bulldozed into the landfill and people's lives become displaced and ruined.

      d.   Agricultural lands are now producing yields far beyond its natural ability due to genetic modifications of plants and the chemical replenishment of topsoil. The problem of top soil erosion from wind and rain, inadequate or improper crop rotation, insufficient time for land to remain fallow, and the elimination of indigenous plants which reinvigorate the soil will steadily decrease the arid acreage required to feed the bludgeoning global human population. Inefficient irrigations methods wastes billions of acre feet of fresh water, and the run off into streams, rivers and lakes contain pesticides and other chemicals that are harmful to both human and animal life. Scientists may be soon called upon to make new soil from rock or from volcanic magma to replenish the world's topsoil. As we now drill for oil, someday we may have to drill for magma once most of the world's topsoil washes into the oceans.

e.   Global warming and depletion of the ozone layer over Antarctica and most of the Artic appears to be accelerating; but since few humans can survive in those areas anyway, too bad on them. The beneficial effects of the natural ozone layer as a shield against UV light are thought to protect humans, particularly light-skinned people, against the harmful effects of sunlight, which can increase melanomas of the skin. The fear lies in scientific extrapolations that show the ozone depletion to be accelerating, which may in the not too distant future expose large portions of the southern and northern hemispheres to excess UV rays, and in addition contribute to global warming as greater quantities of sunlight would reach the lower atmosphere as the ozone layer vanishes. Certain climatic consequences of global warming portends the sinking of great seaport cities such as New York and the complete disappearance of many islands and atolls, such as Tahiti, Bora Bora, and parts of Hawaii. Projections have been made that claim the rise in the oceans depth by upwards of 10 feet over the next century. And that means good-bye to Malibu beach and multimillion-dollar views.

f.   Endangered species have become a hot topic of controversy between developers who don't care what has to die to allow them to profit from new construction, and bleeding liberals whose environmental agenda can sometimes become extreme, unreasonable and impractical. In general, ecosystems are in a dynamic balance between all life forms, from bacteria to plants, insects, and animal species. In any particular environment, there is likely to be found thousands of species of plants, insects and animals. Development reduces the size of an ecosystem, and removes portions that may result in detrimental effects on the natural codependent food chain. Endangered species that once thrived are forced into smaller habitats, which are then threatened by further development. But to stop all development due to one or two little known species can be an extreme and impractical position.

Environmentalists must demonstrate why any endangered species would be incapable of adjusting to developmental pressures before all development is automatically stopped, particularly on private lands. Perhaps developers can provide funds to relocate endangered species to similar habitat or breeding grounds on protected public lands. And if the introduction of an endangered species into habitats that allow them to flourish, but which eventually challenges the populations of competing species, then consider the consequences as a balance in the Darwinian world, of the survival of the fittest. At least the endangered species will no longer be endangered.

g. Wildlife diversity enriches our lives. Imagine a world that is devoid of all wild animals, and their progeny only survive in zoos! We would live in a world filled with pigeons that poop on your roofs, sidewalks and vehicles; domesticated cats and dogs; livestock bred for slaughter houses; and sea gulls that feed off open landfills. What a world that will be for our grandchildren! Global poaching has already placed many of the world's majestic wildlife on the endangered list, and in many cases, the results will be irreversible.

Each year, the world loses thousands of species of living things and along with them, possible cures for diseases and food sources for indigenous populations who can neither afford or desire to become modernized and westernized. Imagine someday once most wildlife have become extinct, our lives will be surrounded only by robots and virtual reality, which would make videogame players happy but would that be life anymore?

h. Ice caps are melting away. The glacial landmass at both poles is receding on the average of a kilometer per year. Large chucks of Antarctica the size of small towns fall off its ice shelves and become shipping hazards in the southern hemisphere. When the poles melt away, the oceans will rise and there will be uncertain climatic changes, such as increased frequency and severity of hurricanes and other horrible cataclysmic events.

i. Space debris is becoming a threat to space travel, whether military, scientific or future commercial explorations. NORAD is barely able to track the 40,000 identified pieces of space junk from the size of marbles to basketballs. Blasting off on a future rocket plane trip to a foreign land may come with dangers from ballistic space junk that travels in excess of 17,000 miles per hour, which is far faster than a speeding bullet, able to penetrate the thin skins of space vehicles and tender flesh of human space travelers. Why is it that human beings are so effective in polluting any environment, from land to water, to air, and now space itself! Nothing is sacred anymore, not even the heavens. The universal belief in mankind's religions and mythology has been the existence of gods from the heavens... could they be extraterrestrials from outer space?

3. Agricultural Reforms

a. Topsoil erosion threatens to decimate the world's food supply. Vigorous planning and agricultural land management must recycle and interchange agricultural and grazing lands to extend the availability of arable soil. Proper crop mixes, alternating crop species, and introducing beneficial insects and animals to replenish topsoil nutrients are essential to preserving our agricultural lands. Natural topsoil preserving plants should be planted and alternated with croplands to improve topsoil retention and recovery. If top soil erosion continues unabated worldwide, scientists may have to invent methods to recycle trash, demolished homes and animal/human waste to restore top soil or people and livestock will eventually consume protein and vitamin fortified synthetic foods that will be manufactured from pulverized wood pulp, weeds, insects and animal parts that are flavorized and textured to mimic vegetables and meats. Yummy!

b. Water consumption in developed nations is wastefully obscene. Although fresh water use and consumption by people, particularly in cities account for approximately ten percent of water use, over 90 percent of that goes down the drains and toilets for hygienic purposes. Should the world's weather change dramatically or enter into lengthy periods of drought, not only will agriculture be threatened, but people will be forced to decide between bathing or drinking water. Extrapolating the human population growth rate into the next 200 to 500 years, it is clear that an insufficient amount of annual rainfall at current rates will be able to sustain the requirements of humanity. Scientists will likely develop water treatment and reclamation technologies, which will be supplemented by oceanic desalinization to make up for the shortfall of rain water; however, distribution will be uneven and costly. New methods of waste disposal and hygiene will need to be developed that do not require the use of water. Hands will be irradiated and blown clean with disinfectants, and disposable scented antibacterial towels and wipes would replace showers. Toileting will involve biodegradable tissue that will be collected and recycled with excretion to be used as fertilizer and topsoil replenishment. Water will be rationed, costly, and made only available for cooking and drinking needs. Car washes will be required to use recycled and/or reclaimed sewer water or subject to fines.

    c. Pesticide usage is rapidly becoming replaced by genetically modified crops to better withstand natural pests. The increased use of cross-species and cross-phylum gene splicing may eventually have unintended consequences on both the environment and on
human reaction to cellular uncertain and unpredictable genetic changes. It is not beyond the realm of possibility that genes taken from certain bacteria or insects may create new food borne diseases that become pandemic and are drug resistant. Anything is possible.

    d. Genetic modifications of plants and animals portends the eventual genetic modification of the human genome, first for improving "natural" immunity and life span extension, but acceptance for eugenic purposes will become sufficient justification for childbearing. The push for knowledge, species improvement and human evolution will push the scientific envelop to perfect cloning and species enhancement techniques. As societies become more tolerant, experiments with cross species genetic engineering and transhumanism will create new human species such as homo canines. Science fiction or future reality? Only time will tell.

4.   Population Control

a.   Abortion is a hot divisive topic between extreme Christian fundamentalists, abortionist lawyers and atheists. Why can't we have a mid-ground that won't require the abandonment of "Roe vs. Wade" in principle? What has fired everyone up is the fact that late term abortions is actually murdering preemies, who might otherwise survive outside of the womb, independent of any drastic life support. How many preemies have survived incubators to become normal children? Lots and lots do every year... way too many! So why should we allow women, on the notion of a right to control their own bodies, have any indisputable right to kill another living human being? Let's allow abortions only up to the point the human fetus no longer looks like a tadpole or lizard. When it's human head, legs, fingers and toes are evident; it's a genuine human without primordial gills, but actual lungs! Aborting a human fetus is murder. Aborting a tadpole is not murder. The pro-lifers argue that every fertilized ovum has a human soul; but have yet to prove that as a fact. If that's the case, potentially billions of human souls are flushed out with menstrual cycles every month. Let's be reasonable. Aborting tadpoles is okay. Aborting humans is not. Pregnant women who are irresponsible should not get a free pass and easy way out. They should be required to give birth, and then have the option to surrender their babies to eager couples who are not capable of childbirth. It could be possible that after 9 months, these pregnant women may choose to keep and love their babies.

b. Legal limits must be placed by governments on the number of children their population may be permitted to add to the global overpopulation boom. China has a one child per couple policy, which has slowed down their growth rate (instead of the 1.3 billion people that they currently have, they would have already attained more than 1.6 billion people, had their government did not enacted a population control policy during the 1980's). India and parts of Africa are prime examples of poverty and suffering caused in most part by out-of-control population pressures. India will soon become the most populated nation on earth, growing from 1.1 billion to more than 1.5 billion people by the end of this decade, while China will grow to 1.4 billion. Africa, despite its AIDS pandemic that claims more than 30 million lives each year, will grow from 850 million to 1 billion mostly impoverished and uneducated tribal people by the end of this decade. China's rapid economic rise is in large part due to smaller more economically manageable families, because less mouths to feed equates to more money in the bank. Overpopulation is a global problem that strains limited resources such as food, energy, water, oceans, forests and pollutes the entire ecosystem due to greatly increased development consequences.

In nations where existing and growing population pressure has a serious and pernicious pressure that results a severe deleterious effect on food, healthcare, natural resources, wealth production, and self-sufficiency; a population control policy must include the mandatory sterilization of every fertile man and woman who has already reached a maximum quota of producing two offspring. The resulting mortality rate will eventually exceed the birth and survival rate, which would lead to population stabilization and reduction. Subsequent to a nation's attainment of self-sufficiency and the ability to adequately provide for its population in all major humanitarian areas, population quotas may be relaxed, such that certain beneficial segments who are capable of affording to properly care for and raise children may permitted to have up to 3 children before forced sterilization. Population control is the most serious and fundamental contributing cause of all of the world's major problems, from environmental pollution to over consumption of food, water, and energy, to species extinction and ethnic/religious conflict and wars. Solving the problem of overpopulation will automatically reduce the intensity of human and global problems on almost all fronts.

The Concept of the traditional family unit as the sole nuclear survival group has changed from the traditional father, mother and children structure to other alternatives. Single parent households in the US now challenge the traditional family setting. Divorced second family unions and combinations, gay couples, foster parents, group homes, juvenile detention centers and adoptive settings now account for the vast majority of non-traditional family settings. The children of non-traditional lifestyles are raised in many cases not having had the benefits of the emotional stability, affection, and responsibilities that have characterized family life in the traditional family setting. However, sociological studies appear to observe that the experience of children raised in non-traditional settings, though oftentimes challenging, unstable and wanting have not resulted in the creation of particularly maladjusted adults.

c.   Schools have become the substitute parenting institutions for tens of millions of children who return daily to dysfunctional, conflictual, and violent home environments. The pressure and scapegoating placed on the teaching profession, as the panacea for all of society's behavioral problems is unreasonable and poorly placed. Students must be exposed to parenting and child development courses to enable them to improve their lives as adults before they are doomed to commit the same mistakes as their parents. The over emphasis on learning the "3 R's" does not make for a more civil or educated populace, because it is the rational application of factual information within a strategy of practical decision making that improves the lot for all. Students should be given credit for any program where their participation to improve the lives of others, whether younger children, their peers, the elderly or disabled serves to better their communities.

d.   Environmental impact is a simple issue with complicated interactive causes, almost entirely the consequences of human activities resulting from population growth, dietary preference for eating livestock, industrialization, development, and modernization. The air we breath is often saturated with harmful chemical contaminants and particulates; the water we drink is polluted by industrial runoff; the ice caps are melting; the oceans rising; deforestation has lowered the average amount of life-giving oxygen in the atmosphere while increasing levels of carbon dioxide that contributes to global warming; and wildlife extinction is only the tip of uncertain consequences that may be the products from the lost of biodiversity. Will comfort and greed oriented humans, particularly the power and economic elites, be persuaded to conserve and change their voracious ways? Not likely, until it's probably beyond the point of "no return" and the long-term damage is irreversible. My hope is people will wake up before the cascade of negative environmental consequences will portend the mass extinction of life on this planet, including homo sapiens – in which case surviving anthropologists will be compelled to reclassify human beings as homo ignoramus.

5.   Religion and Intolerance

    a.   Extremism is the result of incomplete and erroneous understanding of religious dogma, coupled with hatred and dissatisfaction of opposing or competing religious ideas. When people are satisfied with their personal beliefs, whether religious, philosophical, or mundane, they need not compare themselves and their beliefs to others. They can simply practice what they preach, which in religious terms almost universally translates to worship of their God and treating their fellow human beings with respect and kindness. Unfortunately, the history of mankind has been torn by religious conflict, particularly from the three major religions that claim Abraham as a common ancestor. When we look behind the zealous rhetoric behind religious wars, we usually arrive at the economic and political basis that drives jihadists to blow themselves up, or compels superpowers to invade other lands. Let's face it; were everyone to have plenty, with full stomachs, they'd be more interested in resting like lions after a meal, than in fomenting violence. Usually, certain religious, political, and economic leaders benefit from the hidden agendas that motivate extremism and religious conflict. There's lots of money, power, prestige, and even land to be gained from warfare and conflict, and those who perpetuate hatred and misunderstanding have long positioned themselves to milk these sacred cows. Actually, the world should be more peaceful with organized religion, but it hasn't. Why not?

b. Traditional intolerance and hatred appears to be a second nature to most human beings. Is it a genetic predisposition to differentiate, separate, stereotype and show prejudice, bigotry, fear and hatred of those who are not similar to us? Perhaps among the earliest tribal bands of humans, avoiding others meant surviving potential attacks; but that was long ago, right? Nowadays, differences provoke misunderstanding, ridicule, hatred, superiority, and disrespect. Racial, ethnic, sexual, mental, cultural, and political labels and insults abound. Let's name just a few more familiar in the bigotry jargon: nigger, Chink, Jap, gook, fat ass, fag, bitch, dickhead, lard ass, beaner, honky, redneck, raghead, camel jockey, turban head, "butterface" (everything looks good, "but her face"), retard, and so on in probably every language on earth. Wake up call to all Neanderthals! Every human being alive today is a direct descendant of a tribe of Africans who ventured out over 50,000 years ago, resulting in the migration and changes to human DNA to the point races, ethnicities, cultures, and civilizations rose. Why must we hate each other so much on the account of superficial categorizations? Grow up people!

c. The use of violence is universal, as depicted in ancient cave drawings, buried in the tombs of Pharos, unearthed in anthropological digs around the world, and recorded in the history books of almost every nation on earth. Crime, conflict, violence, rape, pillaging, warfare, invasion, destruction, killing, murder have been part of the human experience well before Biblical accounts of Cain killing Able. Violence was a natural survival reaction that kept humans alive amidst hostile and challenging frontiers filled with hungry predators that were higher in the food chain than slow and fragile humans. It was through inventions that homo sapiens rose to the top of the food chain within a relatively short time after the demise of the woolly mammoth, and humans have used the technological edge to kill and subjugate their fellow human beings over the eons of time and civilizations. Will we eventually see the rise of a kinder and gentler human race? The jury is still out on that.

d. Hypocrisy is something everyone accuses others of practicing, but forgets to look in the mirror at themselves. If people were to practice 100% what they preached or claimed to believe, and operated 100% in truth, honesty and the facts, there would be more trust, less confusion, deception, and conflict in the world. Everything would be transparent as people would have to recognize their own faults before attacking others for the same.

6. Capitalism Reform

a. Limit on greed is needed to stop the rape of entire national treasures and populations by the marauding bands of CEOs who head the world's largest multi-national corporations, banks, and military industrial complexes. Currently, the top 10 percent of the world's population own or control over 90 percent of the world's resources and wealth, with the top 1 percent owning over 50% of the global cache, and less than 100 people combined owning 10% or more of the world's wealth. These individuals are the hidden hands behind the world's governments and military might. They manipulate powerful leaders by the use of money through bribes, kickbacks, gifts, political contributions, and even providing free travel and accommodations, booze, drugs and women. They make even the apparently strongest willed and principled to succumb to greed and self-interests.

It's been said that the problem wrong with socialism is socialism, but the problem wrong with capitalism are the greedy and unethical capitalists. Unless capitalists begin to alter their profit paradigm from one of "charging the highest price possible for the least amount of product", also known as the market price, or the highest price the market will bear, the world's wealth and resources will continue to be disproportionately sucked into the vast and insatiable fat vats and secret bank accounts of the wealth elites. It is highly likely that at some "critical point", where "critical mass" is attained by the faceless masses, the current system of capitalism without social responsibility must give way to ethics and a global redistribution of wealth; otherwise the masses will go on rampages and slay the elites through rebellion and revolution. That's the history of the rise and fall of ideologies and civilizations.

Capitalism's main weakness is it creates a tempting and corruptive environment for the most efficient practitioners of the economic system by allowing predators free reign to exploit consumers without restraint and through fraudulent accounting and investment schemes that permits the corrupt to extract untold billions of investor and workers' funds and stash the cash in offshore numbered bank havens to conceal their ill gotten funds from tax and public scrutiny.

b.   There should be a universal law to limit the net appreciation of any personal wealth to be capped at 10,000 times the gross annual wages of the average worker. Any wealth in excess of the wealth cap must be reinvested into non-profit programs and businesses that benefits the society at large (not special interests). Consequently, if the commons improves, then the wealth of the elites should improve; however, the wealth of the elites must no longer result from the greedy exploitation of the working class. We must however place controls on the proliferation of foundations created by the wealthy elites to shelter their monies from taxes, who otherwise do little charity work – at in proportion to the taxes they escape paying, contribute much less to society and its infrastructure.

It is fundamentally inhumane and a great injustice to consumers for capitalists to earn vast sums through the manipulation of accounting procedures and records, mega-mergers that create monopolies and oligarchies which gives them the power to fix prices, and moving labor markets to improve their profits, while destroying the economic viability of entire communities, towns, cities and counties. Unrelenting greed as a "means-ends" justification can only lead to the eventual demise, bankruptcy and downfall of any civilization. The historical outcome has been the same in all nations where greed, corruption, and exploitation have reigned for a time; revolution! If the dynamics and cycles of history continues to repeat, then the days of capitalistic greed will one day be overthrown by the populace, perhaps sooner than later.

c.   Emphasis on tangible wealth versus intangible wealth is necessary to provide the basis for true wealth, and to protect against bankruptcy that appears to occur cyclically when risky and or corrupt investment schemes and strategies are successfully used to defraud innocent investors of their life savings. There is no logical reason why people should invest in companies whose sole product is based upon an illusory pyramid comprised primarily of moving paperwork around or transference of wealth via Internet schemes. Solid businesses of the past had more than half of its valuation based upon tangible assets, such as land, equipment, patents, vehicles, and ironclad contracts. Nowadays, companies are commanding 50 to 100 times their profits to earnings ratio, where their only tangible asset is a website hosted by a server that is connected to the Internet. Once most Internet companies go belly-up, there's little if anything to auction to help investors recoup any lost.

d.   Stock market reforms are long overdue to protect institutional investors and John Q. Public against stock market abuses, insider trading, accounting fraud and corruption.
No wonder once the transference of wealth occurs from the tens of millions of poorly informed investors, the stock bubble usually bursts (usually due to insider manipulation) once CEO's cash out their stock options and leave the average workers, retirement funds, and public investment portfolios holding the empty bags. It's already happened too many times in recent stock market history, and the manipulators have made and continue to rape hundreds of billions of dollars from investors, yet the greedy suckers (gamblers) keep coming back for more punishment.

The stock market is structured to benefit the greedy CEO's, Boards, stockbrokers and the stock exchanges, and is designed to suck money out of the pockets of average investors who are baited by the potential of relative wealth, which statistically has proven to be nothing more than a pipe dream and a deceptive illusion for the vast majority of investors who failed to sell prior to the cycles of bust such as the dotcom and mortgage fiascos.

e.   Corporate accounting reforms are urgently needed across the corporate world. Were all corporations required to adhere to accounting principles that are typically taught in college level introduction to accounting principles courses, investors could rely on the honesty of "the books." Instead, accountants have been permitted to "invent" new and deceptive accounting categories that are solely designed to hide or confuse assets, gains, losses, depreciation, appreciation, and profit in order to transfer wealth away from the view of investors expecting a dividend, or to manipulate the price of stock on the "Big Board." The government needs to do much more to regulate what has become an out of control deceptive and self-serving stock exchange brotherhood.

f.   International monetary system and banking reforms are long overdue, which have kept the vast majority of the world's population in poverty and squalor. The control of the banks is greatly concentrated in small groups of bankers whose heritage continues thousands of years of money lending. Their primary purpose is to enforce a system of banking where the wealth of the masses are in the aggregate loaned and directed to perpetuate the financial and political agendas of its network. Only they know the true value of money from nation to nation, and they use the IMF and World Bank to create unjust and harsh economic policies in developing debtor nations. Their manipulation of governments and economies are almost universal, and they alone hold the power to bankrupt the world system or any member nation, if they found it to be their advantage. The near collapse of the Asian monetary system in the 1990's caused by one of the elite investment banking and hedge fund predators is only one instance where these international carpetbaggers have demonstrated their collective international power to globally realign the wealth of nations.

Now, in this era of electronic banking where digits are instantaneously exchanged, and no tangible assets ever change hands, it would be possible for the international bankers who are the gatekeepers of the international monetary exchange system, as well as private non-governmental owners of the U.S. Federal Reserve Bank system, to artificially create wealth and manipulate computer records and software to increase their digital wealth, while deflating and depleting the national wealth of billions of people with one key stroke. That probably hasn't happened yet, but there isn't anyone who is watching the foxes, because almost all of the executives from governmental watchdog and regulating agencies are staffed by people who themselves come from the banking industry, whose primary purpose is to protect the solubility and profitability of the banking industry. We will all be doomed, once they decide to pull the plug or to artificially add more zeros to their side of the banking ledgers – without any method of detection. Perhaps neo-ambassador Leo Wanta's claim to $4.5 TRILLION deposited in a TRUST with Bank of America and CitiBank is in fact not the profit from the investment of $300 Million from the U.S. Treasury under the auspicious plot of President Ronald Regan to destabilize the Russian economy. Perhaps the principal balance of $27.5 TRILLION held off shore in a Trust (of which trillions have been loaned to various international banks worldwide) is all artificially manufactured digital funds that has been created by crooked accountants as part of an international banking conspiracy – and not the result of Boris Yeltsin allowing the Jewish oligarchs to rifle the Russian treasury and siphon off its gold reserves. In fact, if we do the simple math – the Russian treasury and its economy did not possess $27.5 TRILLION at any time in its history, so while some money was obviously stolen from Russia (perhaps hundreds of BILLIONS), there's no logical way to account for TENS OF TRILLIONS except for MASSIVE CONSPIRATORIAL FRAUD. If in fact Leo Wanta was able to parlay $300 Million in U.S. Treasury notes into a massive $27.5 TRILLION principal, upon which he claimed to have derived $4.5 TRILLION in profit – what the hell did he invest in with such an amazing rate of return on the initial $300 M? If it sounds too good to be true, it probably isn't – and something smells very FRAUDULENT.

g. Limits on MNCs, monopolies and oligarchies are essentially non-existent. The historic Sherman Anti-Trust Act has now become another powerless parchment collecting dust in the Smithsonian Institute, not unlike the U.S. Constitution, which has been essentially rewritten by our federal legislators and Supreme courts in the past 100 years. Every year, mega-mergers reduce competition and create a monopolistic business climate, where consumers are left with choosing the least of 2 or 3 evils. Take a look at the television industry, where only 3 mega-corporations control 90% of the channels in all major markets. So-called regional "Baby Bells" have now merged with larger holding companies who also control competitive technologies, such as cable and wireless, further reducing consumer choices. In almost every field where substantial profits can be made, acquisitions and mergers have decimated the number of survivors in a shrinking marketplace. The growth of oligarchs is certain to accelerate.

      h.   Social responsibility and ethical considerations may sound antithetical to the notion of a free and unregulated capitalistic market system based on the natural fluctuations of supply and demand. And if the marketplace is truly pure and subject to natural market conditions, the issues of social responsibility and ethics would probably not need to be championed. The fact is markets are usually manipulated by regulators who respond to the needs of the very marketeers they are supposed to protect consumers against. This set of foxes watching the chickens presents ample opportunities for collusion, corruption and unethical business practices that are contrary to social justice and the public good.

      Since we can not rely on the corporate world to usher in a marketplace reforms, then one day the exploited masses of faceless consumers will likely wise up, and will form powerful consumer unions, associations, and groups to contest and dog corporate CEOs and corrupt political appointees on regulatory agencies. The light must emanate from consumers who stand to benefit or lose to the greed of corporate executives, because the vast majority of greedy corporate profiteers operate in the wasteland of insatiable greed, where the ends justify the means. The end game of capitalism should not only be bottom line profits, but instead should be integrated with the economic health of the host nations where corporations are housed, not only where they are headquartered.

A capitalistic system where the arms and legs are routinely bashed and chopped off will eventually cause other parts of the body to feel the pain, and will cause great migraine headaches for all those who inhabit the capitalistic head. The adage is, take care of the hands and legs (workers and consumers) to maintain a healthy body (economic system), which will ensure pain free profits for the heads of the capitalistic system. Otherwise, once gangrene sets in, chopping off the hands and feet will leave the body immobile and the head will suffer from stagnant and deteriorating conditions.

7.   Legal System Reforms

a.   Equal access and representation by competent counsel is essential for ensuring justice for all, not only for those who can afford good lawyers. A system that is based upon the rule of law must be fair, transparent, and unbiased to minimize the incarceration of those who are falsely accused and to ensure that the guilty are appropriately punished. When wealthy defendants are capable of paying millions of dollars for the best legal defense, what chance do average citizens have against a prosecutorial system that assumes guilt; and legal loopholes in complex litigation are available to those who can afford it. Without true objectivity, legal intent for delivering justice, and true fairness, the legal system loses legitimacy before the eyes of the public. Without legitimacy, the respect for law breaks down, and the citizenry may rightfully avoid following laws that they discern as being unfair, prejudicial, unethical, and just plain stupid or wrong. All defendants should be entitled to affordable competent counsel, not just overworked public defenders.

b. Internet juries would solve the problem of depleted jury pools. All case materials must be made available for review by the general public on the Internet. Juries may review testimony and evidence via the Internet, along with video testimony of witnesses and plaintiffs (faces obscured to protect their identities from intimidation or retribution). Public Internet polls, briefs, and opinions could be made available to consul to improve their defense strategies and to the prosecution to improve their presentation. The resulting transparency of the legal process will ensure that justice will be done, while increasing the potential pool of jurors beyond those strategically chosen by lawyers and prosecutors who seek biased jurors who are sympathetic to their respective positions.

c. Open courtrooms via television and official Internet websites could act to remove the mystery from the judicial process, thereby improving the general public's understanding, acceptance and support for the rule of law through a system of impartial courts. Video of confidential courtroom participants, witnesses and jurors would be obscured to protect their identities from revengeful and crazy people.

d. Limits on injury awards, which are based upon formulas that fairly compensate victims for actual and future losses should cap the maximum awards that juries or judges may give as compensation for injury. The extra punitive assessments must be eliminated to stop the hemorrhage and greed that extreme multimillion dollar awards cause, which result in the reinforcement of a litigious citizenry and wealthy attorneys who push for outlandish monetary awards. For example, if a 40 year old man was earning $50,000 a year at the time he becomes significantly disabled and loses his ability to work, the maximum award should be based on actuary tables that take into consideration his previous health and projects a probable lifespan. If the man was expected to live 30 additional years prior to his injury, then his maximum award may only be 30x$50,000 which equals $1,500,000. Attorney fees would be awarded in excess of victim's compensation, reflecting the actual effort, time and expense invested into the case, so as not to reduce the value of the victim's award. A person who was earning $1 million per year would be entitled to $30 million in this example, and not one cent more. This would greatly discourage average income or the poor from creating insurance fraud schemes to milk the system, because if they were employed at minimum wage, they would receive a statutory minimum, let's say $100,000 for complete disability, and not $100 million as a punitive judgment against corporate negligence.

e. Lower limits on attorney fees & percentages to reduce the greed factor pursued by most personal injury lawyers. Attorneys should exercise an ethical responsibility to pursuit of the truth and justice, and not just high attorney fees. If they know their client is guilty, they should tell their clients that they think they should plead guilty in exchange for a deal; however, if clients don't admit guilt, then attorneys will make every effort to implement a competent defense. The courts should set the attorney fees for all cases before it, within a range according to a sensible scale that is agreed upon between the legal profession and lawmakers.

f.   Justice and intent of the law is often obscured by the myriad of redundant and conflictual laws that have been written on multiple levels of bureaucracy and governance. Police commonly inform arrestees that "ignorance of the laws is no excuse," yet no one alive is capable of knowing all or even most of the laws that are on the books, with thousands more added every year. No review is made of old, inappropriate, unjust, redundant, conflicting, or just plain stupid laws, many designed to benefit special interests over the public good. A federal agency empanelled by law scholars and retired judges should review all proposed new laws, prior to it being signed into law to ensure that the public good is protected, the intent of the laws are just, and the laws are reasonably enforceable without prejudice to any particular group of the citizenry. In addition, prior to laws being enacted, there should be a mandatory posting of the entire text of the law on the Internet for public review, comments, and criticism for a period not less than one months time.

g. Disengagement of non-violent criminals from penal system is essential if we are to turn the corner from graduating incoming non-violent personal use drug offenders into drug pushers with a propensity for violence and other unlawful activities through the network of contacts that they make while incarcerated. Instead of spending $50,000 each year to lock up a person who uses marijuana for recreational, escape, stress-relief, or medicinal purposes; we should spend the $50,000 on treatment, education, and reintegration into positive programs that serve to better our communities. By investing in helping drug or alcohol dependent individuals to overcome their addictions, they can become more useful members of society who work and pay taxes. Consequently, instead of draining government resources, we create law-abiding citizens to contribute to society's welfare.

h. Legalization of minor non-addictive & harmless social drugs to remove the necessity of otherwise law-abiding citizens from having to involve and interact with criminal networks. Millions of people use legally prescribed drugs as ways to escape the pain or boredom of their situations. Millions more, especially our children and teens inhale or use commonly found aerosols and chemicals to get cheap "highs." In either case, the drugs, inhalants and chemicals often come with harmful and lasting physical and mental consequences.

Law makers must come to grips with reality, that is to say that a certain percentage of average law-abiding citizens find pleasure or comfort in certain non-addictive and generally harmless social drugs, such as marijuana and hashish, when used sparingly. Cigarette makers have killed millions of Americans over the past few centuries, knowing the addictive and harmful effects of cigarette smoke and nicotine. Let people grow their own small amount of naturally occurring marijuana for their own personal use, and make it legal. Cultivation, sale and distribution would continue to be a crime; but within the privacy of one's own home, where a little marijuana use harms no one, why should we otherwise make people into criminals? Don't forget the 1930's, Coca-Cola contained cocaine, and no one got arrested for drinking it. The anti-drug hysteria has become overblown and hyped into a greater problem than it would otherwise be, were lawmakers to take a more realistic approach toward use, prevention, treatment and incarceration.

i. Tort reform; elimination of redundant, antiquated, irrelevant and stupid laws should me a high priority. Our law books now comprise enough volumes to exceed the capacity of a dozen complete sets of Encyclopedia Britannica. It is highly unlikely that anyone will ever read, understand, or remember all the laws that are on the books. The wealthy are able to afford astute legal researchers to discover loopholes in the laws, but people of average means don't even know the vast majority of laws exist. Like the burdensome, complex, and conflictual federal tax code, with exemptions and loopholes only understood by the wealthy and tax evaders, other laws have also become a jumble of hocus pocus and confusion to the general public. Let's not forget the primary purpose of laws, which is to protect the public good from predators. Too often, we now have laws, torts, ordinances, rules, regulations and policies that are designed to empower certain special interests groups, raise revenue for government, to protect the jobs of bureaucrats, administrators, politicians, and CEOs, or to punish those whose view are not consistent with social and political norms of the time. The motive of justice and protection of the public is often lost in the quagmire of special interest legislation. Let's simplify the laws, have less laws on the books, and allow the public free and easy Internet access to all laws; otherwise, how can we expect the citizenry to understand and obey the laws of our land? Ignorance is a legitimate excuse when the legal institutions have not made sufficient effort to inform the general public of the "rules of the game." Where is "due process," when the citizenry is kept in "de facto" ignorance of the laws under which they are ruled? Laws have often become the tool to benefit special interests over the common good. Time for a change.

j.   Transformation of street gangs into legitimate "self-help" non-profit associations could be a constructive first step toward redirecting their activities from criminal enterprises into legitimate business enterprises. Any street gang that demonstrably commits to community service, such as painting over graffiti, helping the homeless, and assisting youth recreation should receive government approval, probationary funding, and local oversight as non-profit associations. If we continue to label all gangsters as criminals, and put the entire weight of our policing agencies toward incarcerating their members for any crime, no matter how big or small, then applying the three-strikes law to keep them locked up for life; it's no wonder many would rather kill their potential witnesses, than simply to commit their crime and escape. Let's try to rehabilitate gang members before they become habitual offenders. An ounce of prevention is worth a pound of cure; and when gangsters fall into the cycle of criminal conduct and prison recidivism, a cure may become unattainable.

8.   Sustainable Employment

a.   Sustainable wages are essential to creating a society where people are productive and independent, instead of destructive and dependent. The math is simple; more people employed equals more taxes collected to support the infrastructure of society. The additional bonus is the alleviation of budgetary pressure on governments to provide entitlement and assistance programs to

impoverished groups, as more of the underclass attain self-sufficiency.

b. Personal assessment, career & organizational matching as pre-screening criteria should be available free of cost at the high school and college levels for all students to help them to make informed and appropriate career choices based upon economic outlook and their personal interests, attributes, and assessments. Over 90% of people end up in careers that they had not planned for, but just "fell into" as a consequence of random chance. More often than not, people enter professions for which their personalities and needs are not appropriate, and they end up locked in a career, living desperate lives for a paycheck. In retrospect most people would prefer to work for low wages, than to chase money in a job that has little personal satisfaction. But wouldn't it be great if people could discover their passions, and find employment in careers that paid sustainable wages for tasks they would otherwise gladly do for free? Obviously, worker productivity would hit the ceiling were employees to be happy with their jobs and bosses. No doubt.

b. Universal access to appropriate educational and training opportunities that increase the probability of attaining employment must be an universal standard. Traditional colleges and universities have become ineffective and outdated institutions for preparing students for most jobs. Too many college graduates have attained worthless degrees that ill prepare them for careers, and graduates are often directed by their bosses to "forget everything you've learned in school," because they do things differently in the real world. The big business of education has become an institutionalized employment program for educators, professors and administrators whose primarily want to protect their own turf.

b.   Unless degree programs can demonstrate a clear linkage with probable career employment, those programs should not be accredited. We are selling our students an empty bill of goods to suggest that their degrees will equate to higher incomes over their lifetimes, based upon statistics. Some of the highest paying jobs are in sales, where a degree is not required, and successful salespeople who demonstrate leadership ability easily move right up the corporate ranks. Many of our greatest entrepreneurs have been college or high school drop outs, who then chased their personal dreams and goals. The college path is great for people who want to work for someone, to fit into a faceless organization in a supportive role or function, whether it be technical, professional, or scientific. People who feel comfortable filling in niches, being categorized with titles, and receiving middle-class wages do well to pursue most college degrees; all others beware.

c.   Objective hiring procedures to minimize interview weight is needed to enforce existing non-discrimination regulations, which are tossed aside during employment interviews. The reality is organizations create a facade that they are "equal opportunity employers," because they accept job applications indiscriminately, and are willing to interview most prospective applicants who meet their minimum recruitment requirements, without regards to race, ethnicity or gender, etc. The reality is interviewers seek people who they feel comfortable with, who they believe will fit well into their organizational structure and culture, and consequently they generally seek reflections of themselves and workers who they believe their bosses and co-workers will accept. Interviewers want to screen out persons who may pose problematic circumstances due to potential misunderstandings that could result from cultural, racial, ethnic or personality differences. Of course, they never tell anyone that the "odd" person is out, because it could become grounds for a law suit by the rejected parties.

It's been commonly reported that over 70% of new hires result from "networking," which is an euphemism for "cronyism" and "nepotism" in most cases. Why? Because employers want to hire people who reflect their current organizational culture, and that's why gay employers give preference to gays, black employers to blacks, Asians to Asians, Hispanics to Hispanics, etc. It's no wonder most of Hollywood's top stars, directors, and producers are of Jewish heritage, even if they may have non-Semitic sounding last names due to name changes or marrying out. It's ironic that all racial and ethnic groups who want to avoid discrimination from the majority, themselves discriminate against all others.

Eliminating hidden networking cronyism, racism and sexism in hiring and promotion would ensure fairness in the workplace. It's a glaring hypocrisy that comments and feelings are kept restrained from people's face, but behind their backs, the racial, ethnic and gender slurs occur routinely and regularly at all levels of organizations. The people who often get ahead are the back-stabbers, liars, ass-kissers, and incompetent bosses who get all the credit for the accomplishments of their underlings. More objectively measurable standards should be used to evaluate the contributions of workers, then retain and promote the best, and not the most politically sly and deceptive members. It's mostly because the shit rises to the top that a slew of corporate executives have been caught committing unethical and illegal acts. It's high time to promote ethnical and competent leadership, and not pals and cronies of corrupt executives and managers.

      d. Objective and measurable merit system in promotion and retention is a simple task. First, set performance standards that are reasonably attainable by the average worker. Secondly, keep accurate records on worker output. Thirdly, reward those employees who consistently and remarkably exceed the production norms, both in quality and quantity. Give additional bonuses to employees who others have voted as being particularly helpful to the organization. By removing the subjective evaluation of bosses, and relying on objective measures supported by co-workers recognition, greater fairness and merit will legitimize promotion and retention among the rank and file.

9.   Drug Laws Reformation

      a.   Legalize minor non-addictive recreational drugs such as marijuana to prevent casual users from having to come into contact with criminals, drug dealers and pushers. Personal use quantities should be declassified from criminal penalties if confined to personal residences, and while not operating motor vehicles or machinery, etc.

      b. OTC legalized minor non-addictive recreational can pay taxes that would otherwise be lost because users deal on the black market with drug dealers and criminals. A safer and more regulated approach would be to allow drug stores to sell government approved brands that have limited THC concentration over the counter, with stronger concentrations to be permitted with a doctor's prescription. The government may require user identification into a database, to prevent abuse, fraud, and drug dealing amounts.

c.   Federal compensation formula for victims of hazardous pharmaceuticals should be fair and reasonable, and proportionate to actual loss of health and life. The formula should take into account a patient's illness, expected morbidity, and suffering that would have occurred without drug intervention, and evaluate the benefits of the drugs versus its expected harmful side effects. Where patients were clearly warned of side effects, and pharmaceutical misleading or fraud is not involved, patients maximum awards should be set, depending upon the severity and longevity of consequential injuries caused by errant pharmaceuticals, not to exceed $200,000 for instance.

d.   Minor drug use to be "ticketable infraction" of Health & Safety Laws instead of crime. The problem with lumping all drug laws into the "crime" category is that it presumes criminal intent to harm others. Often times, especially in the case of Health and Safety Laws, violations are a result of ignorance or poor judgment, rather than criminal intent and calculation. Where actions may harm the health and safety of the violator, which clearly does not endanger others, this class of minor drug infractions should be penalized by a ticket and fine. It is stupidity that drives people to engage in risky behavior that harms oneself, but it should not be a crime if it does not result in harming others.

e.   Active pursuit of drug trafficking financiers and drug investment bankers is where major government interdiction should be concentrated. Filling our already overcrowded jails with drug users will never solve the drug addiction problem. The drug trade requires large flows of cash, which can only be invested by and laundered through banks, financial institutions, investment bankers, and shell corporations. Arrest these insulated groups of drug financiers, and one of the three legs of drug abuse and criminality will be broken. Unfortunately, police are directed to hunt down street users and pushers, while the big boys remain anonymous to pollute societies with large shipments of hard drugs. Where do mega pharmaceutical firms obtain cocaine and heroin to manufacture their narcotic prescriptions like Vicotin, Oxycontin, and Tylenol 3? Where do you think all the drugs from the large drug busts end up? Little doubt down the toilet or it would have been showing up in the fishes a long time ago. No doubt many of the biggest names in financing the drug trade are high up in the world of finance, where anything legal or illegal means more profit. As long as they stay behind the scenes, and everyone else does the dirty work, we will be stuck in a drug culture that has an unlimited and replenished supply of drugs. Cut off the head and the body dies. If drug bankers didn't finance Osama bin Laden's drug trade and pharmaceuticals weren't willing participants in utilizing illegal drugs to manufacture pain killers, he would not have had the funds to develop an extensive network of terrorists.

More effective drug rehabilitation programs for addicts in lieu of imprisonment would take the pressure off our policing personnel to permit them to go after terrorists, which is the primary threat to our economy and way of life. Incarcerating 1000 additional drug addicts will not make us much safer, as compared to rehabilitating them. Drug addicts make good potential terrorist recruits, because they are known to do anything for a fix. If we rehabilitate them and take them off the streets, they will be off the roster of potential terrorist recruits, repetitive criminals, and high recidivist felons who overcrowd our jails.

      f.   Economic enticements for foreign nations to destroy drug crops must be a high priority. It's no accident that the greatest amounts of illegal drug crops are grown in poor Third World nations, whose economic survival often depend on a few cash crops, including drug producing crops. Americans have developed a formidable appetite for drugs, both prescribed and illegal... we have become a drug-dependent culture. It is unlikely that American's will significantly change their need for drugs anytime soon, whether obtained by prescription or illegally. By giving the needed economic support to help develop legitimate industries in poor nations, they would have less reason to deal in exporting the drugs of addiction and death to westernized nations.

10. Energy Consumption & Conservation

      a.   Development of more cost-effective alternative non-polluting energy resources is possible if initial start up funding is injected to overcome the inertial of starting an industry. As long as we rely on oil and it is plentiful and comparatively cheap, we will maintain our gasoline addiction. But if government and industry work together to develop and harness alternative energies, after the first five years, rapid expansion and increased efficiency and productivity will significantly reduce the cost per unit of energy production utilizing non-fossil fuel technologies. When things are mass produced, the price almost invariably comes down to affordable levels. Computers that once cost thousands of dollars can now be purchased for hundreds of dollars, with highly superior technology from previous generations. The same should be expected with developing alternative energies, where future generations will benefit from high efficiency and relatively low cost.

b. Energy self-sustaining and efficient homes and structures is possible once the cost per unit of energy (e.g. BTU) becomes cheaper than the use of fossil fuels. Let's presume that the efficiency of solar power cells and panels, storage batteries, hydrogen cells, wind turbines, home insulation, and hydro-electric generators will greatly increase and the systems become affordable, with government tax-incentives. We could build homes that have several wind turbines on the rear side of the property, coupled with solar panels and hot water collectors on the roofs or back yards, all linked to rechargeable hydrogen fuel cell batteries buried in the ground, and every time water runs through the pipes or when the toilets are flushed, it generates electricity which is used to recharge batteries. The additional electricity and heat generated by such an energy hybrid integrated home could reduce its power demand significantly, and possibly remove it from dependency on national and region power grids that are subject to periodic failures.

c. Hybrid engines that transform and conserve energy would be possible due to Newton's 3rd Law of Thermodynamics, which shows energy can be transformed and conserved. Why can't scientists and engineers develop hybrid power sources that can conserve more of the energy that is typically wasted? For example, an automobile should have rechargeable hydrogen-oxygen fuel cells to run electric-gasoline hybrid engines. In addition, wind turbines built into the underbelly could produce electricity that is used to electrolyze water, which creates hydrogen and oxygen gases, which could be inducted into the cylinders and fired up instead of gasoline vapors. The heat from the engine, engine exhaust pressure, and revolving wheels can all be harnessed to produce more electrical energy to drive the electric motor and other electrical systems, such as the lights and air conditioning. This may appear as a simple view; however, improved technology can pave the way to highly efficiency engines that transform and conserve otherwise wasted energy.

      d.   Improving freeway traffic pattern flow, particularly during long commute rush hour traffic will save billions of cubic feet of pollution and millions of gallons of wasted gasoline each day as a national total. There are too many cars on the freeways, interspersed with slow moving truck traffic and poor drivers. One solution is to limit the number of trucks that can be permitted on the freeways during rush hour, reduce the number of freeway entrances to those that are properly engineered to allow a safe and speedy merging, and removing people from the freeways who live within street commute of their places of employment during rush hour. Each vehicle must have a transponder that identifies their eligibility to be on the freeway during particular times and days. Violations would automatically result in fines, as sensors along the freeway corridors will automatically identify the violators. If people are not headed for work at least 15 miles away from their place of residence, then they don't need to be part of the freeway congestion during rush hour traffic. In addition, people with slow reflexes should be banned from freeways as they are a risk to everyone.

e. Development of more efficient fuels and engines is possible, where an integrated engine would have the capacity to adjust to different fuels and gases. Most gases, when compressed, become superheated and volatile and almost any oil can be used to generate explosive vapors that can be used in the internal combustion engine. Alterations to the common gasoline engine would permit use of alternative fuels, such as kerosene, cooking oil, animal fats, or whatever. Engine temperature can be used to create steam that can drive a supplemental turbine, and electrolyzed water can contribute hydrogen and oxygen gas for fuel. Wheels can become electric turbines and wind speed can be harnessed also.

f. Reducing dependence on oil is essential for several reasons. First, oil has proven to be ecologically deleterious, polluting the air, water, and healthfulness of urban centers, and possibly contributing to global warming. Secondly, best estimates indicate we have perhaps 40 years of oil reserves left in the entire world, if demand and production remain at current levels. It has been theorized that we should have reached the peak of the half-way consumption curve in the year 2000, but industry analysts who serve the oil industry constantly update scientific projections with new optimistic estimates. The fact remains that developing nations such as China and India, which account for almost half of the world's population will continue to increase their demand for oil and energy as a consequence of developmental pressures. This increased demand will at some point soon outpace the producers' ability to produce, and as a protective measure to conserve their remaining national treasures, oil prices will have to skyrocket. This outcome is inevitable as the current speculative oil futures market has shown (with the oil brokers profits). The developed world has become slaves to oil and oil company conglomerates with excess influence on world governments.

When the day of reckoning comes, and vehicles, industries, homes, and businesses have no alternative source of energy, nations will be brought to their knees as prices will soar. It's even possible Islamic clerics and terrorists could by then take over governance of oil-rich Middle-East nations that are now ruled by autocratic regimes who are friendly to the modernized world. But Islamic fundamentalists have little need for oil or money. They want to have a simple life to worship Allah. The average Moslem, unlike Jews and Christians, are not interested in comfort, money, convenience, and social achievements. If they eventually control the oil producing nations, they will likely cut off or seriously reduce oil production. Then the developed world will be tempted to invade and take over the oil. How this war for oil scenario will play out in the long run will be clearly illustrated by the events in Iraq, as the outcome of the insurgency and terrorism in Iraq will demonstrate to Islamic fundamentalists if America and the westernized world has the fortitude to fight a prolong war for oil. In the worse case scenario, the developed world would have to use the neutron bomb to take over rich oil fields. Better that the world should be freed of this burden and potential life ending threat.

11. Political and Ideological

    a.   Ban on political contributions from special interests groups and lobbyists will eliminate the temptation of money to corrupt politicians through special favors legislation. No longer will elected officials feel obligated to appoint those whose members contribute to their political campaigns. Instead, politicians will become beholden to no one, except to serve the general welfare of the people, based upon humanistic, moral and lawful principles. The trust in politicians, elected and appointed public officials, and in government will be restored and we will have more responsive, responsible, transparent, and honest people in one of the most important profession of our time.

b.   Ban on television campaign ads which tend to be negative, misleading, deceiving, and filled with false, twisted, or fraudulent claims. The only people who benefit from political ads are the CEOs of the news media and television conglomerates, who rake in many hundreds of millions of dollars every four years. The public receives jingoism, rhetoric, and very little substantive and relevant facts from political ads. They should be banned unless factual.

c.   Equal access on federal elections Internet website to replace erroneous and divisive political ads, which only insures that the political machines which are best able to raise the most television ad money stand any chance of election. Every eligible candidate must be given equal space on a government approved and sponsored elections Internet webpage. Voters and potential voters should be encouraged through their places of employment, newspaper and magazine ads, by universities, community organizations, and churches to educate themselves about the issues and candidates by viewing the authorized election website, where no false claims or lies would be permitted. No more manipulation by negative ads and slanted news stories. Informed and engaged voters ensure that our budding democracy will continue to evolve and flourish, and will prevent the rise of demagogues who owe their allegiance to the elites, and not to the people. Secure Internet voting to eliminate voter fraud and extensive inefficient voting precincts.

d. UN & US, etc. to recognize universal principles of self-determination based upon national sovereignty, race, ethnicity, and religion. The natural order appears to create nations, cultures, and civilizations around common ancestry, race, ethnicity, ideals and religion. Nations must not go to war against each other based on any of these factors, because it would be the imposition of foreign forces to intervene in the natural evolution of people and nations. If the people in a nation desire a religious based government, versus socialism or democracy, their will must not be impeded. No nation should be required to trade with any other nation. No people should be subjected to having their cultures bastardized in the name of consumerism and modernity. Many non-destructive cultures of indigenous people have been decimated, and their contributions to world peace and natural ways have been forgotten and replaced by the modern paradigm of consumerism, ecological destruction, globalization, corruption, and warfare.

e. Support for universal individual human rights comprised of freedom, liberty, and the pursuit of happiness must be the universal goal of all governments. These ideals are consonant with all major world religions in the respect that expression of such human rights are for the betterment of humanity and the world. Legitimacy must necessary share at the minimum these inherent basic human rights; otherwise the wealthy and powerful will once again place humanity into slavery, suffering and exploitation.

f.   Removing enticements from the Military Industrial Complex (MIC) and international arms trade to create and benefit from global conflicts and warfare. The MIC should be given enticements to tool up for space exploration; let's make rockets to carry humans to Mars and beyond to expand our knowledge, rather than more missiles with nukes for global destruction. In the name of profits, we can do much better than delivering destructive products based upon cutting edge technologies. Let's give the MIC the funds to build better spacecraft and enhance the survivability of our astronauts, thereby reducing the temptation to support conflicts that eventually blow up into large scale conflicts and wars.

g.   It sure stinks at the top! Ethics and not corruption and conflict of interest are essential for good and legitimate government. One of the most important occupations in life should be public service with the goal of bettering society. Unfortunately, too many people enter politics and become appointed to head important government agencies because they have a need for power and their sense of importance comes not from serving the public good, but in making policies, rules and regulations that control and punish the populace. On top of this twisted notion of policy making, many elected officials and agency heads respond to the regular temptation of special interest lobbyists who attempt to purchase influence by corrupting politicians, elected, and appointed officials with various enticements, not limited to kickbacks, guarantees of future employment, and other scandalous self-benefits. When our government officials serve in a cloud of special interests, their purpose to serve the public good becomes tainted as they increasingly become the spokespersons for special interests, whose typical goal is to make profits with little or no regards for the public good, ethics, or public trust. While rank and file employees are criticized for stealing company time through unauthorized routine personal use of computers and phones and occasionally stealing pens and office supplies, high level administrators and executives routinely deal with the devil in corrupt scams that hurt the public and divert funds away from programs that could solve society's problems.

12.   Public Education Policies

     a.   Lowering of mandatory "general education" age limit to 14 because almost all building blocks and fundamental knowledge are already achieved by this age; the typical high school curriculum is a regurgitation of material that should have been properly learned and committed to memory during formulative years. Forcing teenagers to re-learn the same materials is boring and often results in higher drop out rates, that if otherwise challenged with more "electives," practical information, and reality-based subjects, more teens would develop a potentially life long thirst for discovery and knowledge. There are many teens who become experts at computing and programming, who surpass their teachers' abilities with new technologies, yet the school systems continues to utilize old and outdating teaching methods that do little to motivate students to think for themselves and to make good decisions about their own lives. It has been repeatedly demonstrated that idle minds make for active hands, and it's no wonder so many unchallenged and bored teens turn to destructive handiworks.

b.   Mandatory "trade" or "career" emphasis and job training for ages between 14-16 will better prepare teens for adulthood responsibilities. Education should not only be theoretical, but the information should have practical applicability in the real world; otherwise we are failing to prepare our youth for a lifetime of work, learning, and responsibilities. If we don't instill practicum in addition to curriculum, how can we expect our teens to build the habits and knowledge of the working world that they are expected to master upon matriculation and graduation? We teach them to cut up frogs in basic biology classes, but don't give students any practical knowledge on how to cut up chicken into pieces that can be easily cooked. We teach students about acceleration and inertia, but fail to give graphic examples of its demonstration as the outcome of car crashes. We teach human anatomy, but don't discuss how exercise and dancing are interactions of interdependent systems in the human body that seeks homeostasis. Unfortunately, students are left to discover the true realities in life after school, because school knowledge is generally information with little applicability in their daily lives... and it shouldn't be that way at all.

c.   Voluntary education after age 16 and age of consent is crucial; otherwise the extra years of irresponsibility and weaning weakens our youth's self-image and demotivates them from becoming masters of their own fates. In most nations, particularly in the Third World, a 14 year old is already expected to take on responsibilities for working and helping their families. When they display sufficient maturity, they are permitted to marry and to raise families. Discouraging work and responsibility between the ages of 16 and 18 serves to retard the development of a sense of personal motivation, goals, maturity, and social responsibility for oneself and their surroundings. This extending play period is not healthy because the majority of teens at this age, particularly females, have matured both physically and emotionally and are ready to take on the full fledge self-image as adults. As long as we treat them as kids, they will act like children. If society prepares them for self-sufficiency and grants them the rights of adulthood, there will be far less teens in trouble, locked up in prisons, and escaping into hedonistic binges of booze, sex, and drug abuse. Every individual matures at different rates, depending upon the interaction of their genetic predisposition and their family/social environment. Anyone who feels they have attained intellectual and emotional maturity should be allowed to demonstrate their capabilities through various measures. If they pass the tests, they should be considered matured and responsible adults. Certainly, our blood thirsty society considers 10 year old children as adults for incarceration and possibly the death penalty when through their immaturity and poor judgment, they commit heinous crimes. Yet society won't allow our teens to embrace the social responsibilities of adulthood. There's some blatant legal and social hypocrisy there. Let's set aside traditional ideas and norms regarding maturity, and change to a reasonable paradigm that could work.

     d.   Greater individual choice in the selection of coursework and specialization will enable students to feel empowered and engage them in a personal educational process that will have life long benefits, both to themselves and to society at large. Students tend to do poorly or fail classes where the subject matter is not interesting to them personally; and to excel at those subjects that interest them. We should allow students to develop a passion for discovery and knowledge, a motivation that can only be nurtured by allowing personal choice to alter the educational plan, replacing a mandatory read and rote school curriculum that has consistently proven itself to fail most of our students. Our students are consumers of educational products, and they should be allowed reasonable choices as consumers and not have forced education jammed down their throats. If we continue to force feed facts down our children's throats, they will develop stomach aches and heartburn instead of mental insights. Let them think for themselves and make informed choices from the beginning and not only at the end of the educational process, and they will bloom like the prettiest flowers in well irrigated educational soil.

      e.   Elimination of "required courses" that are not applicable to students' career plans allows students to concentrate on developing expertise in areas of their interests and passion. We insist that our students receive a broad and general education, covering the breadth of human knowledge; but in real life, the best paying careers require expertise and specialization. The body of knowledge has increased on geometric proportions since only a generation ago, and the amount of information we expect our students to learn and retain has generally exceeded their attention span, memory capacity, and interests. We need to reduce the number of required courses, and increase career related classes to improve motivation and the development of expertise that is required by our rapidly changing technologies and world.

      f.   Greater use and integration of on on-line courses still drags far behind its potential due to career and turf protection that is endemic to the educational industry. Why must students be forced to learn all coursework in classroom settings, where other students who are either bored, attention-starved, or poorly behaved can reduce the learning opportunity for quieter students? It's been 60 years since the beginning of the Internet, and about 20 years since the personal computer made the Internet available to average people, yet its use as an educational tool has been painstakingly slow. While entertaining and socially stimulating at times, the Internet has been relegated to on-line shopping, auctions, chat, email, porn, and dating. Instead, the Internet should be the universal link in cyberspace between eager students and dedicated professors worldwide, bringing a broader and more realistic educational forum to students at-large. The software and hardware have been in place for the past decade; however the greatest resistance to embracing and fully utilizing the technology has come from the educational sector for fear of losing their jobs. It is now possible for renowned professors to lecture on their subject fields, and have millions of students interact with other professors who can work one-on-one to explain the concepts to those who need additional help. Wouldn't education improve when every student has equal access to the best minds in the human race, and not be limited solely to teachers who are good at babysitting disruptive students with behavioral problems? Let's embrace and fully utilized the technology of learning. Instead of a few slow MAC computers in each classroom, every student should be assigned a lap top with access to all the major research databases in the world. And when computer miniaturization reduces lap tops to card size, then there will be no excuse for ignorance.

g.   More appropriate and world-class curricula is essential to augment and harness the basic power of the 3 R's. Every human predicament requires the use of at least one or two of the 3 R's to provide constructive solutions. After students achieve competence in the basics, which is typically attainable by age 12, curricula should be advanced which challenge students to apply their basic knowledge in logical and strategic methods to problem solve, or to create innovative concepts. Let's emphasize thinking in addition to learning, as both are essential parts of the other. Without the one, the other withers.

h. Universal educational standards that make sense are urgently needed. The current body of curriculum specialists have generally missed the boat on the type of knowledge that is essential to build a better world, happier and more fulfilled human beings, and lessen violence and warfare in the world. They seem to feel that knowledge for knowledge sake is sufficient justification for forcing facts down the throats of our youth, our futures. It is not enough to educate. Education must be appropriate, useful, practical, and fulfilling the purpose of improving individuals and humanity; otherwise why bother. We might as well return to the Dark Ages if what is being taught does little to improve the lot of humanity.

13. Mass Media Reform

a. Strict code of ethics for openness and truth in reporting is necessary to minimize the biased reporting of news bites. It's a fact that Jews own or control the top television networks, newspapers, and magazines; consequently they alter the perception of reality by editing what the public sees, reads and hears. Undereducated individuals and the public at large are judged by media moguls to be stupid and not particularly discerning of the difference between facts and fiction. Generally, the media reports what they want to report, unless the public demonstrates otherwise. Since the media giants remain at the top only through the payment for expensive commercial time by advertisers, they are forced to give the public what they want from time to time. The media giants bet that most Americans are brainless and easily deceived followers who are gullible and fail to investigate facts. No wonder political ads have been the favorite fund raiser for networks and politicians. There is no responsibility for factual representation, as campaign ads routinely present biased interpretations, misstatements, exaggeration, false or misleading information to supposedly stupid and gullible voters. Newsbytes are also manipulated by biased news editors to pander to viewer share; consequently they concentrate and thrive on controversy, scandal, bad news, and horrific stories. Rarely do Americans hear the unbiased facts that they need to hear as responsible citizens and voters.

      b.   Instantaneous public feedback to studios and government agencies on programming is essential to let the networks and regulating agencies know what the public feels is good or bad programming choices. Simply stating that viewers have the choice to turn off the TV or change stations is not enough justification for poor, shoddy, destructive or morally destructive programming. The public airwaves should benefit society, not destroy it.

c.   Elimination of misleading and deceptive television commercials must be an obligation of both advertisers and television studios. There is no innocence for the sake of money-making if the public is routinely being mislead by "bait and switch" advertising or false advertising that convinces the public of "added value" that doesn't exist to the extent that is being represented. Television is not simply an entertainment medium. As an intrusive technology that impacts every level of people's consciousness in the privacy of their homes, with long-lasting social conditioning of developing children, the television industry has an inherent obligation to provide beneficial programming as the litmus test for broadcasting. The airwaves are not free, if the price to be paid is the degradation of our civilization and way of life through the constant barrage of mindless, escapist, negative, sensationalistic and superficial brain programming garbage that panders to market-share as the sole criteria to justify advertising expenditures.

d.   Break up of media conglomerates into smaller diverse independent ownerships is over-due because too few CEO's, editors, producers, and tycoons make the choices for the American public on what they may see. Commercial television has become a perverted wasteland of illusory snippets with little substantive meaning or socially beneficial results. The public is subjected to a series of experimental programming, to ascertain what will attract mindless consumers to stay tuned to their televisions, instead of living life through other more positive activities and interactions. Season after season, it's ridiculous sit-coms with artificially created situations and circumstances that probably doesn't exist in the real world; or its "reality shows" which depict outrageous and perverse circumstances that rarely if ever occur naturally in people's life experiences. With commercial paid time running at almost half of programming time, we have reached a point where viewers are subjected to more advertising than useful programming, particularly between the hours of midnight to dawn. Talk shows that showcase celebrities, biased and controlled newscasts that repeat the same sound bytes, video and verbatim news copy does not serve the public's need and right to factual and useful information. More competition will ensure a broader, more creative and diverse, and more television and news programming, which in both the short and long term will benefit and improve society at large.

14. Recognition of Human Specie's Place in the Universe

    a. On the time line of the known universe, the earliest theoretical hominids are arguable no more than 4 million years old, a recent arrival on the 12 billion year old time line since the Big Bang Theory (or since God created the universe from nothing, some would cite). On the time line of Earth's history. The ancestors of modern humans has been traced back to one African female who lived approximately 100,000 years ago, and all of the races on Earth evolved from the early migration of a handful of tribes from South-eastern Africa some 50,000 years ago. Dinosaurs roamed the world over extended periods in excess of 300 million years and certain species of insects, plants and marine life have been around for hundreds of millions of years, having survived several cataclysmic meteor strikes on the Earth that caused the extinction of dinosaurs. The planet Earth is itself approximately 5 billion years old.

    b. Human value to the existence of Earth's biosystem.

Without a doubt, human beings have become the most destructive force on the Earth's biosystem. People and their activities have directly caused the extinction of millions of species of animals, plants, fish and other non-human life. Over the course of the millenniums, humans have repeatedly killed off their own members in great numbers during wars of conquest, rape and pillage. The relatively infantile human race now possesses the power of widespread thermal nuclear war, which would essentially render the planet inhabitable for a thousand years by most land animals, including homo sapiens. A planet once plush with natural flora, vegetation, forests, wildlife, and teaming with life on every biological level has become greatly denuded of the diversity of what was once naturally occurring species of living things. The beauty of nature has been replaced in most part by concrete, asphalt, farmland, pastures, subdivisions, and landfills. Where proud native and indigenous people were once able to see beauty as far as the horizon, nowadays, few can ever enjoy a clear view through the smog and haze; not that what they would see in cities could ever rival the natural bounty that had once existed, but is now gone forever.

    c.   Value to the evolution of the Homo sapiens species. Humans have demonstrated itself to be both a curious species and a fearful one. On one hand, humans are capable of rising to great challenges in attempting to discover nature's secrets and laws; however, on the other hand homo sapiens sapiens fear of the unknown has retarded the potential of greater discoveries and application of nature's principles. While humans have taken great strides in technological development, little progress has been made internally in the mind and heart of the species. Greed appears to be the primary motivator for the world's leaders and economic elites. Honesty has become illusory in most relationships, where even written agreements and laws are constantly contested in the courts. In many respects, humans appear to be devolving into the Middle Ages, when fear, ignorance and violence once ruled. Geneticists have now deciphered the entire human genome, and the potential for great strides in human engineering exists. Stem cell therapy could become the panacea for most degenerative diseases in the future. Wouldn't it be great if our progeny could be genetically modified to enable self-propelled flight? Imagine a world where gasoline-guzzling vehicles would become extinct because people would be able to run and fly as fast as the birds and wild animals. What would happen to racial, gender, ethnic and religious prejudice when our fellow humans would look alien and be enhanced to accomplish great feats, which could enable deep space travel? We have yet to experience the potential wonders of accelerated human evolution, which would be founded on the creation of great diversity and new sub-species of human beings.

      d.   Human value to the existence of the universe. No doubt the universe would not miss the demise of our species. Our radio waves now have emanated almost one hundred light years into our small galaxy, the Milky Way. By the time any evidence of our civilization could reach potentially comparable intelligent life within our galaxy, we would likely have already destroyed ourselves. Are human beings capable of surviving even another one hundred years, or will greed and conflict doom homo sapiens to an early extinction? Only time will tell, but there may be no one left to hear about it.

e.   Human extinction; blight or blessing? What would the world become, were human beings to become extinct? No doubt, vegetation would eventually cover even the tallest skyscrapers. Mold, bacteria, insects, and a great abundance of biodiversity would again flourish in every corner of the Earth. The polar ice caps would stop melting as the green house effects of human development and maintenance ceases. Great schools of fish would again swim the oceans, as roaming wild animals would regain their natural abundance in rich grazing lands filled with the balance of nature. The skies would again always be blue, cloud filled, and the rising and setting of both the sun and the moon would be spectacular sights. The world would again be teaming with life. Viewed from the moon, Earth would again be a jewel. Oh, what a wonderful world that would be.

The human potential is for greatness, as our wonderful minds and bodies possess. As a species of intelligent beings, we know what we must do to ensure our survival on this small planet. We possess the technology to improve the living conditions of every person on earth, while cleaning up and protecting our natural environment. We possess the natural resources, if appropriately distributed to ensure that every human being will have adequate shelter, food, and medical care throughout their lifetimes. We possess the ability to create meaningful employment that permits individuals to develop self-respect and sustainable lives. What holds us back is the same genetic traits that first helped early humans to survive... fear, clannishness, prejudice, greed, power lust and violence.

As a species, our primal genetic code has not evolved much over the past 50,000 years, since new races evolved from Africans. The primary changes have been superficial and insignificant, primarily the color of hair, skin, and eyes; which have become the greatest source of division and conflict due to wars based upon ethnic and racial conquests. On the inside, humans are almost indistinguishable from each other. No human has wings or gills that actually function. Our skeletal, muscle, pulmonary, excretory and circulatory systems are structured the same, and function exactly in the same way for everybody. When we, as an enlightened species finally come to grip with the destructive nature of greed and warfare primarily to service greed, then humans may stand a good chance to embrace a bright future among the planets of the universe, as we are designed to do.

A NEW GLOBAL ECONOMIC PARADIGM OF SURVIVAL AND HOPE

An economic paradigm shift is possible, where global economic prosperity is a goal within reach, as the rich become richer and the poor become middle-class. History clearly shows that societies with healthy middle classes are economically, socially and politically stable as middle class people are maintainers of society. The economic wisdom of the past and present states that life is a "zero-sum game." This economic model suggests that there is a limit to resources, and conflict arises as a direct result of distribution hierarchies and that create great disparities among the world's populations. The wealthy global elites own and exploit world resources, as poverty envelops the majority of the world's population. It's a matter of history that the zero-sum economic model has created much turmoil, as civilizations conquered, plundered, and destroyed other cultures, only later to meet their own demise. As greed and the zero-sum game model interact, artificial shortages are created by those who hoard, to the detriment of those in greatest need. The zero-sum game of "greed versus need" has resulted in a world where the downtrodden and powerless are willing to fling their lives into destruction, with the hopes of destroying perceived symbols of the ruling class of wealthy elites. History also has clearly shown that the poor revolt against the rich when they have nothing else left to lose. Warfare has almost always resulted from a combination of greed or destitute and wanton greed has been the motivating force that has had a highly disproportionate effect on destroying our little planet.

A new economic paradigm that recognizes abundance must envelop the world order to eliminate the seemingly perpetual zero-sum game paradigm. We need not look too far to discover that life, our earth, and our universe is filled with limitless abundance! Certainly, there exist sufficient natural resources to support a reasonable human population of less than ten billion people, if resources are properly exploited and distributed. Management and distribution of world resources should eliminate waste, conserve the ecosystem, and intelligently use natural resources through technological enhancements to solve even the most persistent and perplexing human problems. The rich, who can provide capital and skills to optimize world resources, can become richer, as poverty is eliminated, and a growing global middle-class becomes the consumers of production that is owned by the wealthy elites. It's a win-win paradigm that can be utilized to improve our environment and to save for world for the future.

It is essential to examine the basic premise that created and perpetuates the zero-sum game mindset. During humans' earliest times, each day was a struggle for survival, as food, water and other usable natural resources appeared to be limited and in short supply, often requiring hoarding and defending. As civilizations and nations evolved from tribes and city-states, the fear of shortages continued, as human conflict, violence, and warfare sought to distribute the seemingly limited human resources to the powerful, creating a class of wealthy individuals. In today's world, nations struggle to protect their "national interests" as globalization of economic structures by multi-national corporations and the wealthy elites threaten to subjugate the economic interests and survivability of poorer nations. The zero-sum game continues to place large armies face to face across imaginary boundaries, waiting for the order to attack, destroy, kill, and plunder. Conflicts persist around the world; Korea, Iraq, Israel, Palestine, Liberia, just to name a few, with dozens more "hot spots" festering, waiting to be ignited by competition for the illusory limited wealth in the zero-sum game.

Getting beyond the illusion of limited natural resources, and recognizing the great abundance of untapped potential wealth will not be a simple task. Global coordination, vision, intelligent management, new technological applications, and sensible distribution of resources will be required to raise the global economic tide in a manner where the rich can get richer, as the poor become middle-class. Each continent and every nation possess natural wealth, some discovered and much unexplored that can be transformed to wealth in the global marketplace. Africa, South America, Australia, Canada, India, China and Russia all contain vast undiscovered and unexplored stores of valuable minerals and other natural resources that can be transformed into wealth. Even in the West, a trip through America and Europe easily shows a vast bountiful landscape of unsettled areas, farmlands, pasture, and deserts that contain undiscovered and unexplored riches beyond its present day uses. Human progress and development need not destroy our ecosystem if we utilize eco-friendly and non-polluting processes while eliminating old and outmoded processes that contribute to global warming, species and eco destruction. The potential for new industries that create great wealth and economic growth while protecting the environment is real.

A global eleven-point plan should be adopted by the United Nations to encourage the replacement of the conflict producing "zero-sum game" model with the realistic "abundance" paradigm. These ten points of development identify essential areas ripe for growth and wealth generation from crops, energy, minerals, recycling, and space by harnessing new technologies.

I.   Global Food Production:
      1.   Biotechnology to maximize harvests, control pests, disease and crop failures
      2.   Scientifically improve crop rotation programs to restore land use without laying fallow
      3.   Global computerized coordination of farm production to eliminate duplication and waste

4. Global computerized coordination of distribution and pricing

5. Plant new species of edible nutritious disease resistant crops that require less water

6. Genetically engineer new crops that can grow even in the toughest terrains and soils

7. Develop new farming techniques for harvesting the deserts, mountains, and marshlands

8. Use advantageous insects to increase harvest and control pests and disease

9. Use of advantageous bacteria and microbes to increase harvest and control pests

10. Increase fisheries, supplemented by oceanic seeding to replenish natural populations

11. Breed livestock, poultry and fish that grow faster, larger and healthier that can survive on a wider variety of cheaper grains, or foodstuffs not consumed by humans (e.g. weeds)

12. Genetically engineer heartier livestock and the feed it requires

13. Genetically engineer new breeds of livestock, poultry and fish for human consumption.

II. Global Food Distribution:

1. Food is sold and distributed to continental warehouses coordinated by management cooperatives, corporations, or government agencies, according to global treaties that establish specific protocols and procedures

2. Continental food banks distribute to member nations within its continental boundaries, and to private corporations in accordance to paid purchase agreements, credit/barter
3. UN food charity receives five percent of all food for redistribution to impoverished areas
4. Surplus food is sold to independent distributors for secondary and specialized markets
5. Food prices are managed globally to derive incentive profit for distributors, predictable and steady income to producers, sufficient supplies and reasonable prices to consumers

III. Oil and Gas Production, Pricing, and Distribution
1. Predictable stability of world oil prices through graduated and structured 5-10 year guaranteed production and pricing levels by OPEC and other oil producing nations, with price increases capped at no greater than five percent above world growth levels.
2. Global distribution equilibrium, with wealthier nations and consumers partially paying higher prices to subsidize poorer nations, on a temporary basis according to a global growth plan designed to raise the tide for all nations.
3. Excessive retail profits limitation to prevent price gouging, fraud, corruption, and destructive levels of inflationary greed by middlemen, where any prices exceeding 100% retail mark-up must be redistributed

50% to the producer, 25% to government, with the remaining 25% to the retailers.

IV.   Mineral Exploration, Exploitation and Recycling:
    1.   Existing mineral uses
        A.   Precious metals production should be stabilized to meet demand
        B.   New uses of existing supplies to enhance value of existing minerals & metals
        C.   Clean up coal, oil shale and fossil fuel production and utilization
        D.   Increased use of compressed natural gas for public transportation
    2.   New uses from most abundant natural resources
        A.   Sand, rock and magma
        B.   Geo-thermal vents
        C.   Salt water
        D.   Kelp, weeds, prairie grass
        E.   Smog & air pollutants
        F.   Cow and animal wastes
        G.   Human waste products
        H.   Ocean floors
        I.   Lake and river sludge
        J.   Plankton
        K.   Bacteria and mold
        L.   Insects
    3.   Recycling
        A.   Automated mega-assortment recycling centers that process by the truckloads

B.   Organic sumps reprocessing centers

C.   Biomass and waste reprocessing

V.   Solar:

1.   Energy for commercial buildings and home

2.   Energy to supplement vehicle hybrid engines

3.   Satellite focused energy beams

4.   More efficient solar collector arrays and solar cells

5.   More efficient solar collector batteries

6.   More efficient solar powered motors and engines

7.   More efficient technologies, combining various solar blade designs in hybrid large and mini tower arrays

8.   Compact designs for buildings and urban uses

9.   Vehicle spoilers to convert wind velocity into battery power

VI.   Lightning:

1.   Balloon arrays

2.   Discharge blimps

3.   Lightning rod farms

4.   Lightning "catch basins"

VII.   Hydro-electric:

1.   More efficient turbines at hydroelectric plants located in dams

2.   New technology offshore turbines to harness oceanic waves

3.   New technology turbines to harness strong river currents

VIII.   Wind:
1.   More efficient turbines – design and technology
2.   Expand transmission network to tie into major electrical grids
3.   Identification of high wind areas that are not likely to change due to global warming

IX.   New Materials:
1.   Lighter
2.   Stronger
3.   More flexible
4.   More resilient
5.   More esthetical
6.   Cheaper to produce
7.   Found in natural abundance
8.   New technological applications
9.   New markets created by consumers
10.   Potential for expansive applications

X.   Nuclear
1.   Retrofitting or closing dangerously aged facilities
2.   Upgrading safety with new technologies
3.   Freezing construction of new plants except on military bases
4.   Phasing out nuclear power plants as alternative energies prevail

XI.   Space Exploration:
1.   Mine the moon and Mars (but beware of potential lunar/Martian viruses/bacteria)
2.   Explore and harness our solar system (but beware of potential alien viruses/bacteria)
3.   Colonization of suitable moons and planets

Some of these ideas may appear to be radical, but none serves to threaten the existing economic hierarchical structure. In fact, several areas are currently under development by scientists, corporations and governments. Each area of development offers the wealthy elites vast opportunities to invest in greater profits, as the world's population benefits from the new technologies, materials, and global economic stability that will be spawned. The pursuit of abundance is natural and expansive. The fixation on the illusory zero-sum game model serves only to limit the production of wealth, as it casts billions into lives of poverty. Making the right choice for either progress or continued conflict will determine either the survival or extinction of humans, while generating a vast surplus of wealth for the global elites or fomenting destruction.

The pursuit of abundance will harness the great resources and technologies spent on military defense, and permit those investing in the next war instead to find greater purpose and power by investing in tomorrow's peaceful technologies based upon similar technologies now utilized for weapons design and production. Investing in abundance is "win-win" for everyone; the rich, poor, middle-class, the military, defense industries, high tech corporations, low tech companies, manufacturing sector, service sector, and governments of every nation on Earth.

Nay-Sayers will always offer reasons why investing in abundance is impossible, but they'll be left behind, clinging on to old outmoded models as if the Earth is the center of the universe. Along with this new millennium, we must look to the future, as the methods of the past are behind us, and dragging them along only slows progress and burdens humanity as a whole.
The human species can not afford to make extinction level mistakes due to shortsightedness.

Chapter 5 – The Right Path

(written in 2008 prior to election and recession)

The vast majority of Americans want both Presidential candidates to take the high road toward factual representation and truth. They want both John McCain and Barrack Obama to avoid negative sensationalistic mud slinging. Anything less will be seen as business as usual, and most Americans believe they and all of America deserves better from these supposedly honest men of great integrity. (Note: The electoral mandate is for bi-partisan compromise to solve our nation's problems and to work across the aisle rather than to take hard philosophical stances that result in legislative gridlock).

The business climate and leadership

Increasing business globalization, technological applications and international competition is creating ample opportunities for multi-dimensional companies to maximize their market niches and earnings. Organizations who are able to rapidly adjust to changing market trends will not only survive, but will also flourish during a roller coaster economy, as less prepared and inflexible companies become non-competitive. During rising economic times, visionary enterprises float to the top of a rising sea, quickly leaving the slower competitors behind. The lack of a realistic vision deprives corporations of their market potential, but organizations with visionary leadership are almost always able to remain on top.

What about people and life?

The vast majority of people usually desire to do what is right. People will pursue activities that appear to give them personal benefits, while avoiding losses; however, the preponderance of individuals are basically honest, who feel it is wrong to cheat and hurt others in order to obtain personal gain. People also need a feeling of belonging and appreciation. They want to be accepted for who they are and to receive just credit due them. If they must be criticized, people want constructive suggestions, with positive intentions, and not be targeted for personal attacks. It is desirable to communicate frankly and openly, and not be too quick to judge others. We all live in communities, whether at home or at work, and we rely on others to cooperate in order to progress in our lives. The exercise of leadership, honesty, kindness, understanding, and forgiveness are tenets of good interpersonal relationships that engender good will to all that serves to improve societies and the world's civilizations.

Unfortunately somewhere around 5% of people living in America do not have our best interest in mind, are not loyal, and are involved in corruption or criminality. We need to reach these people to turn them around to do good deeds instead of evil. Any farmer knows that it only takes one bad apple to spoil the entire box, given sufficient time. We need to develop a sense of social responsibility to weed out the rotten apples and to wash them clean after removing the bad parts.

Basic values?

Our nation and the world would be a much better place were people to become more accepting, tolerant, communicative, encouraging, listening, learning, teaching, motivating and thoughtful to engender greater trust and positive actions. We need to behave appropriately, honestly, and in a respectful and civilized manner. Public and private courtesy demonstrate personal considerateness, which sets a good example to others on proper conduct that should improve our social environment and society.

We are fortunate to live in a relatively free society, where law and a free press protect our liberties. Patriotism, doing what's right and legal, helping our neighbors, being friendly, and exercising sound judgment and responsible behavior are small goals that each of us are capable of accomplishing on a daily basis. Improving our lives, our families, communities and nation begins with each and everyone of us, and the small steps we take each day will lead to a better world.

The framers of the U.S. Constitution shared a broad but common vision on the foundation of the rule of humanitarian process of governance that has endured for over 200 years, improving with successive generations of American idealism. We stand at another crossroad of generational change that could lead to the development of a common vision of social justice, economic security, ecological preservation, energy independence and global foreign policy. But we now stand on the edge of an economic cliff that could lead to the demise of America as the world hegemon.

With the advent of this new millennium, we entered into a new global paradigm, where interrelationships between bankers and stockbrokers become intermingled with the mutual monetary goals of drug cartels, illegal arms merchants, enemy states, corrupt politicians, criminal syndicates, and international terrorists. The flow of drugs and weapons is often financed by diverting legitimate funds, with illegal profits washed clean through money-laundering networks abetted by domestic and international banks. It has become difficult to track down the financiers of terrorism only because on the surface they appear to be legitimate individuals, usually above suspicion, but occupying high perches from which great financial benefits are derived.

The majority of Americans support our government's effort to protect our homeland from attacks, and even though we suspect no system is perfect, there may yet be times terrorists will be somewhat successful in causing wanton death, destruction, and mayhem. President George W. Bush is the first American president to place our nation on a "proactive" footing with the Bush Doctrine - a political stance similar to the Truman Doctrine to contain the spread of communism, where rather than to wait to be attacked by our enemies first then react after the fact, America reserves the right to strike if facts on the ground clearly indicate the security of the United States is at dire risk. The old adage, "an ounce of prevention is worth a pound of cure" is still very appropriate in our new post-modern high tech era, in our nation's concerted effort to defeat our true enemies (terrorists states who support terrorists). However, as long as the majority of the world's people remain poor and destitute, they are likely to become the fodder and foot soldiers for madmen and terrorists.

Our homeland and military are exposed to many areas of vulnerability, and the problems that have been revealed amount to just the "tip of the iceberg." Mega-greed knows no loyalty to nation, culture, ideals, or people. Greedy people are hypocrites, serpents, and a brood of vipers. To those who worship money, the ends justify the means, and they are fully capable of employing any means necessary to achieve their greedy financial goals. Terrorism, drug dealing, illegal arms trade, mega-corporate mergers, political corruption and investment scams are just the tools that are employed to derive their ill gotten wealth. A house divided can not stand long, consequently as the multi-pronged attacks against fundamental American institutions continue to go unabated, our enemies can greatly weaken America by influencing or controlling key U.S. communication and administrative hubs that could fatally compromise our military, political, economic, social, and international relations institutions and personnel. Our enemies' common agenda is to bring America down.

Globalization and the rapid rise of MNCs, elitist CEOs and oligarchs signal the rapid demise of ethics, morality, humanitarianism and patriotism. We need not look too far to the event horizon to see our potential futures destroyed by international carpetbaggers and terrorists. We must win the war on the secret financiers of global terrorism soon, otherwise it will be too little, too late.

FUTURE ECONOMIC PERILS TO THE AMERICAN ECONOMY
(written in 2008)

Our domestic economy is comprised in excess of 80 percent by service sector jobs, which indicates it is primarily based on people relying on others to do what they lack the adequate skills, time, or desire to achieve. It's an economy based upon an abundance of ignorance, laziness, and conveniences. Common sense would suggest that ignorance, laziness and convenience are not precursors of a competitive economic system in a global paradigm, as compared to economics based upon knowledge, expertise, effort, and perseverance.

The infrastructure and relationships within the American economy may portend an inherent weakness toward eventual and sudden collapse, as artificial stock, employment, and monetary value bubbles burst. Critics would argue that the American economy is the strongest that the modern world has ever seen, with GDP over $13 trillion annually. However, several recent events indicate the U.S. economy is subject to severe fluctuations, such as those which almost bankrupted several economic sectors after the "911" terrorist attacks, in addition to the "dot-com" collapse only a year earlier and more recently the housing bubble bust and hyperinflation oil prices. And more recently the stock market crash and run on the banks have put the American and global economies into great peril – with sharks and predatory perpetrators of the impending economic collapse set to benefit and to become global oligarchs.

Let's examine a plausible scenario based upon current economic and geo-political trends. By the year 2010, with Germany, France, and all European nations will share a common monetary system and Great Britain (UK), pressured by economic necessity, would eventually join the E.U. China's burgeoning growth, coupled with Japan's capitalization has the potential to become a regional partnership powerhouse in Asia, each holding vast sums of American dollars, together producing the majority of products consumed by Americans.

Americans may dread the day when a united EU-UK, coupled with a united Asia, with Russia as a bi-lateral trading partner of both, cooperate to provide economic pressure against the United States. Juxtaposed against this dire economic backdrop could be unrelenting conflict in the Middle-East, as Arabs continue to resist Israeli power and presence in former Arab lands.

The internal economy, upon which U.S. GDP (gross domestic product) data accrues is comprised by measuring the spending of American consumers, government, investors, and net exports. Carving up the $13 trillion annual U.S. GDP indicates that government spending (federal, state, local, etc.) accounts for over $5 trillion, consumerism for another $5 trillion, and investments of about $3 trillion annually (not including the half trillion budget deficit and trillion dollar War against Terrorism) . A projected federal deficit of $1 trillion (not to mention states, such as California's $17 billion budget deficit), and a deepening trade deficit exceeding $500 billion suggests that our domestic economic bubble is comprised to a great extent on illusory spending. The U.S. national debt approaches $10 TRILLION, which rapidly approaches its annual GDP – further indebting future generations to indentured servitude.

It is estimated that over $1 trillion in U.S. currency and bonds are owned by foreign interests, individuals, groups and nations, such as Saudi Arabia, China, and Japan. In addition, many foreign and multi-national corporations (MNCs) directly own or control in excess of $2 trillion invested in American corporations and real estate portfolios. What might happen to the U.S. economy were certain foreign interests to make sudden enormous liquidation of U.S. currency, stocks, bonds, and real estate investments? A rapid spiraling drop in consumer confidence would surely follow such wholesale destructive market movements. In 1997, the manipulation of billions of dollars of hedge funds by a single man greatly contributed to the near collapse of the Asian monetary exchange market, contributing to severe devaluation of the domestic currencies in Indonesia, Malaysia, Korea, and other SE Asian countries. Could a similar scenario happen right here in the United States of America? A large coordinated attack against the U.S. dollar could cripple the American economy, and drive the U.S. into a severe economic depression, with only the treat of worldwide thermonuclear war as a subsequent and real deterrent against foreign economic domination or invasion.

The fundamental question remains; "Does the U.S. have the capacity to survive independently of international trade, were our current trading partners to become our trading competitors or enemies instead?" What could happen if foreign governments such as Saudi Arabia and other oil producing nations were to conspire to "de-dollarize" their oil exports, such that U.S. dollars would no longer be accepted as payment for crude oil? Would the U.S. be forced to drain our precious oil reserves, and then trade our limited gold and transfer military hardware and technology in barter for oil? Certainly, under such circumstances, the U.S. economy would immediately go into shock, with run-away inflation that will create an out-of-control cycle of massive job loss, plummeting stock market values, widespread personal and business bankruptcies, and destruction of capital and capital assets.

Under such a scenario, the U.S. economy would experience a paralysis not seen since the Great Depression of the 1930's, and would call for Uncle Sam to start another round of FDR-style public employment programs to save the economy. But where would the federal government find tax dollars to spend? States and local governments would become bankrupt, and there would be insufficient taxes collected from the shrinking employed population to fund any ambitious government-backed employment program. A precursor of America's future economic problems may be experienced by California (arguably the sixth largest economy in the world), as its bonds were valued just above "junk" by bond rating companies less than 4 years ago. Is it conceivable that U.S. government bonds could also become "junk" someday? Simply printing more money to pay off existing bonds and debts held by foreign investors would not clear the ledger, without causing the complete collapse and rejection of the dollar as a medium of international trade.

Were such global conspiracies among our potential competitors and foes to materialize, what could the U.S. government do to survive, while leading Americans back into solvency? Already, multi-national corporations approach the world as one global marketplace, without any loyalty to nation, creed, or politics. Profit making and profit taking is all that drives the global economy as capitalism without any morals or consideration of future perils. America's largest corporations have taken on the appearance of money-making vehicles to return exorbitant CEO compensation packages, to the detriment of both stockholders and employees.

Corporate profits are often not reinvested back into the domestic economy in the form of stockholder dividends, new hiring, and investment in buildings and equipment. Instead, profits are taken out of the U.S., and hidden in offshore tax-free havens, or invested overseas in nations with low standards of living with abundant cheap labor. How do irresponsible corporate actions contribute to strengthening the American economy? It doesn't, and instead places America in potential economic peril.

Energy Consumption & Conservation

a. Development of more cost-effective alternative non-polluting energy resources is possible if initial start up funding is injected to overcome the inertial of starting an industry. As long as we rely on oil and it is plentiful and comparatively cheap, we will maintain our gasoline addiction. But if government and industry work together to develop and harness alternative energies, after the first five years, rapid expansion and increased efficiency and productivity will significantly reduce the cost per unit of energy production utilizing non-fossil fuel technologies. When things are mass produced, the price almost invariably comes down to affordable levels. Computers that once cost thousands of dollars can now be purchased for hundreds of dollars, with highly superior technology from previous generations. The same should be expected with developing alternative energies, where future generations will benefit from high efficiency and relatively low cost.

b. Energy self-sustaining and efficient homes and structures is possible once the cost per unit of energy (e.g. BTU) becomes cheaper than the use of fossil fuels. Let's presume that the efficiency of solar power cells and panels, storage batteries, hydrogen cells, wind turbines, home insulation, and hydro-electric generators will greatly increase and the systems become affordable, with government tax-incentives. We could build homes that have several wind turbines on the rear side of the property, coupled with solar panels and hot water collectors on the roofs or back yards, all linked to rechargeable hydrogen fuel cell batteries buried in the ground, and every time water runs through the pipes or when the toilets are flushed, it generates electricity which is used to recharge batteries. The additional electricity and heat generated by such an energy hybrid integrated home could reduce its power demand significantly, and possibly remove it from dependency on national and region power grids that are subject to periodic failures.

c. Hybrid engines that transform and conserve energy would be possible due to Newton's 3rd Law of Thermodynamics, which shows energy can be transformed and conserved. Why can't scientists and engineers develop hybrid power sources that can conserve more of the energy that is typically wasted? For example, an automobile should have rechargeable hydrogen-oxygen fuel cells to run electric-gasoline hybrid engines. In addition, wind turbines built into the underbelly could produce electricity that is used to electrolyze water, which creates hydrogen and oxygen gases, which could be inducted into the cylinders and fired up instead of gasoline vapors. The heat from the engine, engine exhaust pressure, and revolving wheels can all be harnessed to produce more electrical energy to drive the electric motor and other electrical systems, such as the lights and air conditioning. This may appear as a simple view; however, improved technology can pave the way to highly efficiency engines that transform and conserve otherwise wasted energy.

d. Improving freeway traffic pattern flow, particularly during long commute rush hour traffic

will save billions of cubic feet of pollution and millions of gallons of wasted gasoline each day as a national total. There are too many cars on the freeways, interspersed with slow moving truck traffic and poor drivers. One solution is to limit the number of trucks that can be permitted on the freeways during rush hour, reduce the number of freeway entrances to those that are properly engineered to allow a safe and speedy merging, and removing people from the freeways who live within street commute of their places of employment during rush hour. Each vehicle must have a transponder that identifies their eligibility to be on the freeway during particular times and days. Violations would automatically result in fines, as sensors along the freeway corridors will automatically identify the violators. If people are not headed for work at least 15 miles away from their place of residence, then they don't need to be part of the freeway congestion during rush hour traffic. In addition, people with slow reflexes should be banned from freeways as they are a risk to everyone.

e.   Development of more efficient fuels and engines is possible, where an integrated engine would have the capacity to adjust to different fuels and gases. Most gases, when compressed, become superheated and volatile and almost any oil can be used to generate explosive vapors that can be used in the internal combustion engine. Alterations to the common gasoline engine would permit use of alternative fuels, such as kerosene, cooking oil, animal fats, or whatever. Engine temperature can be used to create steam that can drive a supplemental turbine, and electrolyzed water can contribute hydrogen and oxygen gas for fuel. Wheels can become electric turbines and wind speed can be harnessed also.

f.   Reducing dependence on oil is essential for several reasons. First, oil has proven to be ecologically deleterious, polluting the air, water, and healthfulness of urban centers, and possibly contributing to global warming. Secondly, best estimates indicate we have perhaps 40 years of oil reserves left in the entire world, if demand and production remain at current levels. It has been theorized that we should have reached the peak of the half-way consumption curve in the year 2000, but industry analysts who serve the oil industry constantly update scientific projections with new optimistic estimates. The fact remains that developing nations such as China and India, which account for almost half of the world's population will continue to increase their demand for oil and energy as a consequence of developmental pressures. This increased demand will at some point soon outpace the producers' ability to produce, and as a protective measure to conserve their remaining national treasures, oil prices will have to skyrocket.

This outcome is inevitable as the current speculative oil futures market has shown (with the oil brokers making the lion's share of the profits). The developed world has become slaves to oil and oil company conglomerates with excessive influence on world governments.

When the day of reckoning comes, and vehicles, industries, homes, and businesses have no alternative source of energy, nations will be brought to their knees as prices will soar. It's even possible Islamic clerics and terrorists could by then take over governance of oil-rich Middle-East nations that are now ruled by autocratic regimes who are friendly to the modernized world. But Islamic fundamentalists have little need for oil or money. They want to have a simple life to worship Allah.

The average Moslem, unlike Jews and Christians, are not interested in comfort, money, convenience, and social achievements. If they eventually control the oil producing nations, they will likely cut off or seriously reduce oil production. Then the developed world will be tempted to invade and take over the oil. How this war for oil scenario will play out in the long run will be clearly illustrated by the events in Iraq, as the outcome of the insurgency and terrorism in Iraq will demonstrate to Islamic fundamentalists if America and the westernized world has the fortitude to fight a prolong war for oil.

In the worse case scenario, the developed world would have to use the neutron bomb to take over rich oil fields. This might be a fear that motivates the Iranians to attempt to develop nuclear weapons. Better that the world should be freed of this burden and potential life ending powers over the waves of globalization as the downtrodden drown in the ocean of despair? Only time will tell as the tools, mindsets and people have already been in place prior to the end of the last millennium. History has clearly shown that it repeats itself in cycles, with the similar catastrophic human consequences. It's not just a matter of "if" - it's simply a matter of "when." The stone has already been cast in the lake of fire. What can citizens and patriots do to contribute to strengthening the American economy? If Americans remain complacent, their futures may well be made by foreign powers who are already hard at work dissecting the American economy.

Some of these ideas may appear to be radical, but none serves to threaten the existing economic hierarchical structure. In fact, several areas are currently under development by scientists, corporations and governments. Each area of development offers the wealthy elites vast opportunities to invest in greater profits, as the world's population benefits from the new technologies, materials, and global economic stability that will be spawned. The pursuit of abundance is natural and expansive. The fixation on the illusory zero-sum game model serves only to limit the production of wealth, as it casts billions into lives of poverty. Making the right choice for either progress or continued conflict will determine either the survival or extinction of humans, while generating a vast surplus of wealth for the global elites or fomenting destruction.

The pursuit of abundance will harness the great resources and technologies spent on military defense, and permit those investing in the next war instead to find greater purpose and power by investing in tomorrow's peaceful technologies based upon similar technologies now utilized for weapons design and production.

Investing in abundance is "win-win" for everyone; the rich, poor, middle-class, the military, defense industries, high tech corporations, low tech companies, manufacturing sector, service sector, and governments of every nation on Earth.

Nay-Sayers will always offer reasons why investing in abundance is impossible, but they'll be left behind, clinging on to old outmoded models as if the Earth is the center of the universe.

Along with this new millennium, we must look to the future, as the methods of the past are behind us, and dragging them along only slows progress and burdens humanity as a whole.

The human species can not afford to make extinction level mistakes due to shortsightedness. Millions of people who immigrated to America after World War II from devastated lands who sought refuge and a new start in the "land of the free" where economic rewards appeared to be proportionate to one's willingness to accept the sacrifices of hard work. Now almost 70 years later, there is some regret that this attraction to the "land of opportunity" may have been a mistake. Europe and Asia have prospered greatly since the War; however, it appears that America may now be positioned for a long slide with its generational long national debt and out of control government spending. If solutions are not found and implemented, many Americans may have to accept a standard of living that is equivalent to that of developing nations.

The consequences of almost 70 years of economic, political, and social evolution has resulted in a fragmented nation, floundering in the tides of time, without purpose and direction, lacking in resolve and self-confidence. Yet, in the hearts of most Americans, there still kindles the great ideals of freedom, democracy, and self-determination; however, the problem lies in an equally great confusion on the definition of constitutional concepts, that have now become another source of conflict and disunity among the masses.

Many Americans no longer know what it means to be "American." Is being American simply worshipping the sanctity of a common flag? Is being patriotic the code word for being anti-foreign, especially anti-ethnic? Ask 100 people on the streets, and probably no more than a handful can list the first ten Amendments to the U.S. Constitution, known as the Bill of Rights.

So who should we blame? The Japanese, Chinese and So. Koreans for the unbalanced trade and resultant trade deficit? Certainly their protective and unfair trade practices have engendered a resurgence of anti-Asian racist attitudes among the American rank and file. But if all things were equal, and each American bought $1 of Japanese goods, and sold them $1 of American goods, there would still be a trade deficit because there are twice as many American consumers than Japanese. The Japanese would have to amass a total disposable income twice that of Americans before they could buy $2 of American goods for each dollar of Japanese goods sold to America. Statistics show that the Japanese in fact buy more American goods per person (per capita) than Americans buy from Japan. The Japanese have invested more than $1 Trilliion U.S. dollars in American bonds, helping to finance our government's deficit spending. China's almost $1 Trillion USD loan was instrumental in financing the bank and American auto industry bail outs when the great recession of 2009 blind sided Americans and the global financial markets. They are also taking heavy losses in their American commercial real estate investments during this latest recession. While American corporations are laying off American workers and opening shop south of the border and in Asia, the Japanese have opened auto manufacturing plants in the U.S.A., hiring American workers by the thousands. Does this sound like the actions of an enemy?

Should America kick out all the foreigners, and keep America for Americans only? That means repurchasing over $800 billion USD in European ownership of America, and over $800B USD in Japanese ownership of America, over $1.3T USD of US Debt held by the Chinese, over $500B USD held by the South Koreans and over $300B USD held by the Taiwanese which is roughly equivalent to all the money our federal government collects in taxes each year (numbers updated circa 2012). And while we attempt to turn back the wheels, why not make international air traffic illegal, and declare all international trade agreements null and void?

Why not nationalize all foreign-owned businesses on American soil, and kick out the aliens. We have enough natural resources to sustain our population indefinitely, and we could aim all of our nuclear missiles at every nation in the world who may be a threat to our xenophobia (because certainly America FIRST!). We could develop a great patriotism and national pride based on a "us against the world" fantasy. The frightening part of this scenario is that millions of Americans would vote for such a platform today, just as sure as the 55% of white voters who once favored electing David Duke, a professed racist to be Governor of Louisiana. During these times of economic downturn, must we resort to extreme and fundamentally un-American notions to solve our problems? I don't think so; however, if the political and corporate leadership continues to bathe in their own needs before the needs of America, then this extremist scenario is inevitable, and the seeds of a second civil war may indeed be sowed. Then the militias may turn out to be right after all.

But Americans don't give up! This is a nation of explorers and malcontents who fight to the end. How we can each help to affect positive changes in our individual lives and especially in changes needed to the self-perpetuating institutions that have fostered a system of mediocrity and failure in America for the past generation? How can average Americans save America?

If the American experiment fails, then perhaps the future of mankind will rekindle the homogenous warring nation-states era of history. And in an age that is already proliferated with nuclear weapons, it would not take but a few zealots and terrorists to touch off the beginning of the end. So it has become even more increasing essential to the survival of mankind that America must recover its confidence and resolve. America must prove that the strength of American ideals enables people from all races, ethnicities, cultures, religions, and gender to share in a fair and lasting prosperity. If America sheds its commitment to individual freedom and progress, then the world is doomed to warfare and possibly human extinction.

This essay was written to the average person, in the hope that the confusion and great mysteries of America may be illuminated, effectuating further questioning, speculation, and solutions. Many of the observations, opinions, and statements are no more than exercises in the expression of free speech and free press, and much of discussion are extrapolations, interpretations, and restatements of common facts reported by the news media. Many people will differ and contest the basic premises of this book. Disagreement is a healthy process if it encourages further discussion and exploration of the available information and perspectives, leading to a rediscovery of questioning. A more active involvement in the search for facts and truth could lead to a less apathetic and more purposeful populace, and result in the involvement and election of more responsible public representatives. Perhaps voters will someday entrust public leadership primarily to politicians who are respected on par with physicians, rather than to people who the general public equate with sometimes unscrupulous used car salesmen or tricky lawyers.

THE AMERICAN ECONOMIC SYSTEM - WHO'S ON TOP OF THE WORLD? (circa 1995, but true today)

America is being raped by the corporate greed of the international pirates that include the leadership of the largest multi-national American, European, and Japanese conglomerates. American executives now earn an average of 500 times the wages of the average worker, even during times of mass lay-offs, large corporate losses, and bankruptcies. The European and Japanese executives earn 10 to 50 times the wages of their average workers, yet they are succeeding, for now. The global community is regressing to a stage of feudal nation-states, where the economic disparity between the ruling classes and the masses once again becomes legitimized by its institutions, where a small minority comprising the wealthy elites exercises domination over the majority poor, and the primary purpose of the consumer classes is to provide a vehicle of profit for the wealthy equity holders.

Despite so-called experts who perpetually disagree with each other, the economy can be explained in rather simple terms and concepts. There are four basic components of any economy; first, natural resources; second, manmade goods and services; third, distribution; and finally, value that is created by demand. When any of these economic elements become unbalanced, the economy skews toward those who controls any of its elements. When any particular group controls the first three components, they develop a virtual monopoly on the fourth. Different political systems utilize laws to alter the natural relationship between these four elements of economy to shift wealth from its unprotected classes (the poor and consumer classes) to its protected classes (the economic and political powerful).

If left alone, without governmental restrictions, except that transactions should be based on a doctrine of mutually fair exchange of similar value (of whatever equivalent method of trade), economic systems would naturally tend to become balanced systems. If you don't believe it, name one person who you know who would knowingly consent to a barter situation where his own interests becomes secondary to making a profit for the other guy. If so, let's just give away the store. But in reality, with the legitimization and collusion of special interest government, the economic interests of the average citizen is subrogated to the self-perpetuating interests of the power brokers who attend to the economic interests of the ruling class, and depend on special interest support to maintain their positions.

Institutionalized inequities are more apparent in certain industries than in others; however it pervades the entire economic structure of America, is legitimized by government, and is taught in universities as the way things should be, further perpetuating a system that primarily serves the will of the wealthy. We will discuss some of the more obviously maligned areas of our economy, and propose some potential solutions to bring a real economic balance to America. (2012 update – the numbers and rift have only gotten worse).

THE MIDDLE CLASS, OR SOCIETY'S NEWEST SQUATTERS?
(circa 1995, but true today)

A redistribution of wealth from the rich to the poor, socialism, returning to a basic barter system, or any revolutionary change in the economy is not suggested. Positive changes should develop in prudent, predictable, and incremental steps to minimize the systemic shock that invariably results in great suffering for the vast majority of people. We should not dismantle all the positive institutions and systems that exist, but instead improve and encourage the development of a more motivated, productive, and wealthy middle class to ensure a diverse economic foundation that can survive in the global economic markets. We need not repeat the mistakes of either the People's Republic of China or Russia. We must not repeat the mistakes that resulted in the Great Depression of the 1930's.

Certainly there is a better way by investing in the middle class. Strengthening the middle class creates consistent markets for more products and services while providing the wealthy class greater opportunities to amass even greater fortunes. The larger tax base enables government to provide needed infrastructure improvements, funds to reduce the federal debt, support of social programs, national defense, and technological advancement expenditures. The shrinking middle-class can have a devastating effect on the economic survival of our nation, and decreases opportunities for both domestic and international businesses. While many cash fluid rich can increase net worth a hundred folds during a recession or depression by their ability to buy property at highly discounted prices from those who are cash starved, the long-term devastation of a recession or depression actually decreases the amassing of fortunes when compared to performance during economic boom periods.

The real causes of economic recession are the imbalances that are created when vast sums of money leaves the country from an imbalance of trade, the exporting of American jobs by both American and internationally-owned companies, and the uncontrolled runaway debt incurred at all levels of the economy, from individual to corporations and government.

Presently, the total net worth of all the property in America has been estimated at $50-55 trillion. The gross productivity of the economy (GNP) is approximately $4.5 trillion per year, and the federal budget about one-fourth of the GNP. Federal, state, and local taxes and user fees now account for about 40% of the average household's expenses. The top 1% of the population owns one-third of all the wealth in America (the top 5% owns almost two-thirds), the bottom fourth owns less than 5% of America, and the middle-class owns the balance (30%). America is rapidly becoming a two-class society, of the rich versus the poor. Mankind's history is filled with examples of civilizations whose governments were eventually toppled by the poor after the disparity between rich and poor become obscene and inhumane. (2011 – Arab Spring and Occupy movements).

KILLING THE GOLDEN GOOSE WITH TAXES AND THE FEDERAL DEBT (circa 1995, but true today)

The federal government has now incurred over $1 trillion in national debt, and pays 25% of its taxes collected annually toward interest payment on that debt, operating on a $250 annual deficit. This amount will grow to over 30% by the year 2000, if not sooner. America has borrowed heavily against its future income, on the expectation of greater future productivity, erroneously based on an aging and retiring population, a decreasing number in the workforce, and decreased industrial output and annual Gross National Product. It certainly sounds like a page out of bankruptcy court.

The possible solutions are basic and must be applied simultaneously. First, more revenue is needed to offset the increasing debt payments. Secondly, expenses must be controlled, wasteful spending eliminated, and greater value for the dollar must be sought for each dollar spent. Third, new borrowing must be severely curtailed, loan repayments restructured over a longer term, and new borrowing to pay existing debts must be avoided. Finally, the dollar must be gradually devalued against other international currencies against an acceptable level of inflation. This will also act to inflate the prices of imported goods, and decrease the relative costs of our exports; consequently, improving our balance of trade, creating more American jobs, and resulting in a higher tax basis that translates to more income for the government to offset the federal debt.

Proposed capital gains tax breaks for the rich must be accompanied by a domestic reinvestment criteria to deter pulling out of profits from local businesses, and further requiring reinvestment of the tax savings into the American economy. Any program of tax breaks designed primarily for the rich with no strings attached will only add to the exportation of American jobs to cheaper overseas labor forces, or adding to investment in non-job producing investments such as antiques, rare coins, and paintings. To move boldly into the future, we must encourage investors to invest in the mechanisms of the future, such as factories and product research, and discourage tax breaks for investing in non-productive commodities such as gold futures, and other non-employment producing articles. (2012 – little to nothing has changed that has institutionalized wealth to the elites)

BANKING ON CREDIT, WHERE DID ALL THE MONEY GO? (circa 1995, but true today)

The explosive growth in the number of failed and failing banks, savings and loans, and other lending institutions is endemic of a failing system based upon a abrogation of basic good economic sense. Banks were initially places to deposit savings and valuables as an added measure of safety and security from outlaw forces. The evolution of banking created corporate entities whose purpose was no longer the protection of depositors' assets, but the reinvestment of those assets for the purpose of making a profit for the investors. Consequently, corporate greed and governmental acquiescence and collaborative guarantees permitted the banking interests to invest in very risky ventures such as loans to third world governments and foreign companies, dry oil wells, real estate scams, and unproven technologies; all with substantive losses that were "written off" the books, meaning the taxpayers footed the bill for billions of dollars in bad loans made by American lending institutions.

Average Americans couldn't get a loan for a business start-up during the same time wheelers and dealers were using letters of credit and loans to raid solvent companies, leaving them straddled in excessive long-term debts. And now, many of those takeovers have resulted in the bankruptcy of the shell of what were once successful American corporations. Of course the corporate raiders have long since run off with their $ billions in profits that have directly resulted in the loss of hundreds of thousands of jobs. These greedy corporate raiders should not have been admired, but rather they should have been jailed, just as the head of the failed Lincoln Savings and Loan was jailed for preying on and destroying the lives of untold thousands of people. Historically, the seeds of the failure of the banking system lies in the special interest influence of banking industry executives on governmental regulators and politicians whose laxities have resulted in a system that is out-of-control, insolvent, and has violated the trust of its depositors. Government makes an ineffectual regulator when its lawmakers and officials implement fiscally irresponsible laws and regulations that have encouraged lending institutions to make highly risky investments that should not have been permitted at all. Now, again the taxpayers are stuck with the enormous expense of bailing out insolvent institutions.

Solutions to the banking problem as another weakened leg of the American economy must first start with an examination of the concept of "credit." Creditworthiness is the cornerstone of lending. An individuals ability to qualify for a loan is normally evaluated against his credit history, and the future prognosis of timely repayment of a loan. The interest rate that is charged to individuals for the use of the lender's money is tied to the level of risk that the lender takes in consideration of a borrower's assets, income, existing debts, reputation, employment and credit history. Somehow, basic lending principles applied to working-class individuals are often disregarded when large loans are made to corporate executives, corporate raiders, large corporations, and foreign governments and entities. We are now learning the lesson that apparent "bigness" does not insure solvency, as

Donald Trump, Carl Icahn, PanAm, and Macys can attest. Everytime a large corporation goes belly-up, untold thousands of workers and related businesses are hurt, and the taxpayers absorb the bill for bad loans made by lenders to large corporations because usual lending criteria and practices that are usually applied to evaluating individuals are disregarded when dealing with the economic elitist class.

The cost of credit is another area that has become essentially unregulated. It was once usurious and illegal for individuals to charge more than 10% interest on a loan (to deter loan-sharking); however, we now find that the biggest loan sharks are institutional lenders, auto financing companies, thrifts, and the government itself. Credit cards at 21% interest, car loans carried by dealers at 24% interest, appliance purchases carried by thrifts at 21% interest; and late payment interests of 25% per year plus 25% penalty for uncollected taxes (that adds up to 50%), and parking ticket fines that are doubled if not paid in full by the stated bail date (100% penalty). Any excessive interest payments decreases the net productivity of individuals. If a man earns $2000, but pays $500 for interest payments, $500 in taxes, and $700 for rent and utilities, that leaves him very little for food, transportation, clothing, and "living". He is essentially broke. He would otherwise be solvent if his debt payment were only half as much.

The biggest scam in credit is the idea of compound interest. If you loan the bank $1000 (when you open a savings account, you are actually lending the bank your money) at 10% interest, you will have $1100 after one year. If you do not touch your money, at the end of two years, you will have earned 10% of

$1100, or $110, for an aggregate total of principal and interest of $1210. When the bank loan your money out, they need to recover the amount of interest that is paid to you, plus an amount for profit. If the bank loans your $1000 out at 15% per year for two years, and schedules level term repayments, the borrower repays 30% interest or $300. The bank makes a $90 profit ($300 income from borrower minus $210 paid to depositor) which translates to 43% on the amount paid to the depositor. Actually, the borrower never has the entire $1000 to use, because he starts repayment after one month. And that amount of money that is repaid by the borrower is loaned out again. That's why deferred payments on auto loans increases the vehicle price by 50% over a 4-5 year period, and the actual price of a home is paid 3 times over a 30 year period (with the first 20 years of payments scheduled primarily to interest payments).

The solution should be the elimination of compound interest, and a reversion to simple interest. If one borrows $1000 at 15% per year, the bank should be paid interest only payments of $150 per year for each year that the $1000 is outstanding, with the principal to be due at the end of the term of the loan. This enables the borrower to actually have the full $1000 available for his use during the term of the loan. In addition, the burden of monthly repayment would become manageable. The borrower would be required to purchase affordable government guaranteed loan insurance, and deposit a reasonable percentage of the loan principle into a government escrow account (this could be the FDIC insurance escrow account). In the event of default, the insurance company and the governmental escrow account makes the bank whole, including interest. The defaulting borrower is assessed a reasonable percentage of the defaulted loan balance still due after security instruments are sold off to satisfy partial repayment of the original loan. Any balance due is divided into payments according to a sliding income schedule, and collected along with witholding income taxes until the deficiency judgment is satisfied.

The U.S. Treasury is political mechanism that is too much under the control of a few. Allowing one man to set interest rates is too much power to give to anyone, and in the future could foster a greater unequal distribution and waste of government dollars by supporting welfare for the rich through manipulation of the value of money and interest rates to benefit specific sectors of our economy, primarily the wealthy who receive various tax breaks and incentives and subsidies. (2012 – one major factor that caused the bursting of the housing bubble and resultant 2009 recession was due to banking scams and creation of the climate for foreclosure when the feds increased interest rates at the same time adjustable rate mortgages were scheduled for rate hikes to their caps thereby increasing monthly loan payments by 50% to 100% when salaries were flat.)

THE STOCKMARKET MENAGERIE (circa 1995, but true today)

A baffling contradiction appears in our economy today, where the stock market posts record highs, breaking the mythical 4000 barrier while unemployment remains high. If we were to count everyone on welfare, homeless, under-employed, or who have given up looking for work, the unemployment numbers would double! Why at a time of great stockholder profits are companies still going bankrupt and thousands are losing their jobs? Where is all the money going? Why are the profits not being reinvested into companies to maintain jobs? Are the wealthy class, armed with inside boardroom information, taking advantage of institutional investors such as pension plans? When counties lose billions of dollars in the stock market game, who is winning those dollars?

Taken as a group, investment experts are no more effective in predicting the future value of stock than flipping a coin or throwing darts blindfolded. Studies have shown that chimpanzees make better stockbrokers than most of the pros. The real money is being made by those with the inside track, friends of corporate management who are leaked insider information, and can make clever buy and sell decisions that is subsequently mimicked by the public sector institutional investors and John Q. Public. The lag in time between insider trading and the movement of large blocks of public sector stock equals big profits for those clever private investors who are able to buy low and sell high. It's a simple case of the horse leading the cart. Of course, our government regulators are blind to it.

When companies first go public, and make a stock offering, investors buy shares of stock to provide needed capital for company growth, on the potential promise of future performance. Depending on the eventual growth of the company, the number of times the stock is split, and the amount of stock that is retained by the company, future stock value may have little impact on providing significant additional capital to companies for additional growth. Shareholders become the beneficiaries of stock profits, and the process of stock trading moves real and paper profits among the various investment portfolios of investors, but may have little beneficial effect on providing needed reinvestment income to companies. The improved value of a company's stock translates into increased creditworthiness, and permits companies to "borrow" capital on the open market, and decreased stock value severely limits a company's ability to borrow money. The irony is that companies that borrow get deeper into debt, and this has a potentially negative long-term impact on the stock value of the company.

We see it all too often. Stock prices go up, investors take their profit out for the short-term kill, without regards for the long-term solvency of the company. Large long-term institutional investors, and the public are left holding the bag. So when the value of the stock market goes up, the slower moving institutional investors and the less informed average investor will benefit along with the stock manipulators (however at a lesser proportionate gain per share); however, when things start to sour, the horse drops the cart and heads for greener pastures, while the cart remains stuck in a gully, and takes the big losses.

The stock market is a macrocosm of an investment club. With investment clubs, individuals pool their capital to support the economic well-being of their investment choices. The basic premise is sound, and provides a means of more rapid economic growth to companies. The hope is that the increased operating capital provided by investors will translate into a company growth rate that significantly exceeds the amount invested, thereby providing a handsome dividend to investors, even after a company assumes additional debt from borrowing outside of the investment group. Without the invention of investor clubs that evolved into the stock market, and the legal creation of the perpetuating corporate entity, the great economic boom of this century could not have been possible.

But are times changing? Is all of this paper profit actually beneficial to the economic strength of American industry, and therefore the nation as a whole? Or is the system set up to benefit the sophisticated mobile class of wealthy investors who move money internationally among the major stock markets, sometimes to the disadvantage of American corporations? Why should our national confidence be based on the health of the stock market? When the market is up, the rich become wealthier, yet the ranks of the poor increases as middle-class Americans find themselves in unemployment lines. This happens because money not paid to employees is reallocated to pay for larger executive salaries and bonuses, and to increase the return on investment to shareholders. When the market is down, employees are laid off to provide savings that again translates to protecting the investors and corporate executives. Either way, the working-class gets shorted. A double blow comes when the market is down, and workers' retirement pension programs that are invested in stocks lose value; and consequently lessens or wipes out their retirement protection.

The solutions are simple. The short-term and especially the long- term health of corporate America, and consequently American jobs, would benefit from the stability that would be created if investors were required to reinvest a significant amount of capital back into the companies to support the infrastructure of the company (improvements in plant, equipment, and workforce) and to reduce the net effect of debt. For instance, if at the time an investor sells his shares, the stock value has increased by 20%, then 20% of that increase should revert to the company's reinvestment fund, leaving the investor a net gain of 16% over the purchase price. This may encourage investors to invest for the long-haul, adding to the stability of American corporations.

Obviously, something must be done to curb the outrageous incoherent compensation plans given to corporate executives without regard to corporate performance. Executives, who are responsible to manage America's industries in a responsible way, should have a particularly high stake in reinvesting a significant portion of their profits back into their corporations. Exercising stock options to take out $ millions from a company, receiving 100 times the salary of the average worker, abusing the company expense accounts, and setting themselves out as a special class of power brokers who wine and dine with politicians, showing little respect to their rank and file workers, and professing other megalomaniac attitudes have only weakened America's economy. Would a good father keep 100 times the average family income for himself, while the rest of the family lives on a near-starvation diet? This is exactly what corporate executives are doing to its own family. And with each American family whose breadwinner is laid off and cast into hardship and self-doubt, having to depend on public assistance programs for survival, America suffers as a nation. And when the welfare pots politically vanish, these disenfranchised Americans will undoubtedly turn to crime, including blowing up buildings. (2012 – obviously the repackaging of mortgages, student loans and corporate debt then making those investments opportunities have inherent weaknesses as the Wall Street bet is to increase the value of such risky portfolios, then for major players to divest just prior to collapse. Investments have often become a house of cards where new investments products are no more than the repackaging of existing investments and adding another level of debt on top of what already exists).

THE CONFUSION OF INSURANCE EXCESSES (circa 1995, but true today)

Insurance was a clever notion that was initially developed for the common good. The concept of insurance was the pooling of money by many to contribute to a common savings to be utilized in the event of disasters for that may be suffered by its members. Like many other once noble ideas, insurance has evolved into another form of legalized gambling (not unlike the stock market). Here again, the public is persuaded to hand over up-front money on a potential promise of future benefit. The public bets that ill-fated events will inevitably occur, and the insurance companies wagers that that death and mayhem will strike only an insignificant proportion of the population at any particular time. And they have scientific data, actuary tables, and other sophisticated methods to prove that they are right.

But the fears of the American public has made the insurance industry one of the most formidable special interest group in America, after the oil industry, agribusiness, and banks. Californians passed a law to require rebates on excessive overcharges by insurance companies, yet legal maneuvering, delays and defiance has demonstrated the true power of the industry, permitting them to prey on the deep rooted fears of the public to make excessive profits while to defying the will of the people.

Ask any widow, accident, fire, or burglary victim who has received an insurance settlement, and they will swear by the goodness of the industry. Ask anyone who pays exorbitant insurance premiums, who has never received (and most likely will never receive) an insurance settlement, and they'll swear they're being ripped off. Both groups are correct. Individuals do need assistance during times of great personal loss. Insurance is a viable method, where the collective assets of a large group can be brought to bear on the losses of a significant few. The problem does not lie in the basic premise. It lies in the implementation of the concept.

"Whole life" is sold as a savings plan, where policy owners may even borrow against their own investment, and pay the insurance companies additional interest payments for the use of one's own money. If one survives the term of the policy, the entire amount invested is returned as a retirement income, plus a small sum of interest. As a savings or retirement plan, anyone would do better to buy U.S. Savings Bonds. When purchasing only the "protection" component of insurance in the form of "term life", the savings portion of a whole life policy may be invested in the bank at an average higher return than is offered by most insurance companies. Rates charged to insure a particular auto or home varies wildly, and depending upon the insurers, rates that target various sectors of the consumer market may differ in excess of 300 percent. Consequently, consumers need to become informed shoppers.

Consumer confusion in understanding insurance policies and the insurance industry speaks well for exploring a joint public-private insurance arrangement. The government should offer insurance guarantees to individuals, not unlike that offered for real estate loan programs such as FHA, Fanny Mae, and Freddie Mac (2012 - but unlike those programs that insured lenders against losses and screwed the consumers). Government would guarantee premium payments during such times that the policy holder is out of work, and unable to meet his monthly payments. This would be especially helpful in the case of providing health insurance coverage to all Americans. All insurance companies would routinely deposit a certain percentage of the collected premiums into an insurance guarantee fund, that the government would use to pay insurance companies for lost premiums until individuals could find employment and are reinsured by their employers.

Employers whose size makes it infeasible to provide health insurance coverage would also deposit a specific amount into the insurance fund based upon their number of employees, and the government would contract out to insurance carriers or public hospitals for major medical coverage. This would encourage a partnership between the government and the insurance industry to provide responsible coverage for its people, and discourage the industry from exorbitant overcharges. (2012 – HMOs were supposed to make health care affordable by managing the spiraling cost of health care. However all HMOs have done has to add another layer of money grabbers interested in profits while doctors and hospitals become their employees as premiums skyrocketed and coverage became inadequately provided. The reality is middlemen positions such as HMOs become gatekeepers and profiteers for doing little except moving paperwork).

THE AMERICAN WORKER, A NEW PERIOD OF SUFFRAGE
(circa 1995, but true today)

The typical American worker has lately been characterized as being lazy and illiterate. Americans work a shorter average work week than the Japanese. So what? Before collective bargaining, corporate abuse of the American worker was severe. Twelve to sixteen hour days and six day work weeks were common. Child labor was a disgrace. Working conditions were hazardous and contemptible. Workers finally exerted their collective voice for humane treatment, resulting in the rise of unions and protective legislation. Much of America's economy growth occurred during a period of unionization.

With the gradual demise of union influence during a period characterized by more responsible employee protection regulations (due in part to unions taking on the similar insensitive attitudes as traditional management, corruption, and lackluster gains for its employees), we have seen a corresponding decrease in worker productivity. When unions were active, workers felt a sense of banning together for common goals, to demand fairness from management. The sense of camaraderie created a pride that translated to a reputation for hard work and quality products. Widespread employee rights legislation took the thunder out of the union movement. Why should workers pay high union dues to obtain the same benefits and wage increases that would be provided by employers without bargaining units? After President Reagan fired all of the air traffic controllers who were on a union strike (and banned them from future federal employment), the public realized how ineffectual unions could be. Unionized workers who stuck the Los Angeles Herald-Examiner newspaper never received a raise, nor got their jobs back. Instead, the paper eventually went out of business. These absolute attitudes of non-compromise and disregard for unionized worker rights by government and big business send a strong message to the American worker... if you strike, take a hike.

The American worker was steadily becoming demoralized. Job security was no longer a viable concept. It would not be uncommon for workers to experience unpredictable and periodic lay-offs when various sectors of the economy would experience recessions as the indirect result of political, corporate, and international manipulations. Technology has rapidly changed the face of the American work place, realigning the biological clock to the pace of computerized mechanisms of work, from the office to the assembly line. The workplace is becoming a dehumanizing experience. It became unlawful to express personal opinions, and the exercise of the freedom of speech often resulted in punitive sanctions by the employer or governmental agencies. Workers not only had to worry about job security as a function of economic factors, but had to be concerned about the idle things they said at the workplace that might be interpreted by people as being sexist, racist, or anti-gay, etc. Interpersonal relations had to suffer as a people became reticent to expose their true feelings.

While restraint may have had a superficial effect of smoothing over relations at work, a deep undercurrent of estrangement, alienation, and demoralization of the American worker has developed, often leading to greater long-term stress-related problems, even causing violence. Worker dissatisfaction statistically translates to increased absenteeism caused by on-the-job injuries, illnesses, personal leaves; and consequently a decrease in productivity. To make matters worse, executive compensation was often at the expense of worker layoffs. Let the workers eat cake (or worse, as President Reagan had considered "ketchup" as a food in proposing a cut in the federal food stamps program for the poor). An attitude of let the workers be damned, and blame the workers for America's economic woes was fostered by many who attempted to focus attention away from the real causes of America's economic problems... corporate greed, decreased reinvestment in the means of production, overextended credit debts, exportation of American jobs, control of economic factors by a minority of the wealthy elite, and politicians who feel more responsible to special interests than to voters.

The American worker built this great nation. When the American worker is healthy, the nation's economy is healthy. When the American worker can not earn enough to be the mass consumers of the products of industry, then the economy will suffer. If corporations can not sell their goods, then they too will suffer. Each dollar earned by a typical worker is recycled in the internal economy 7 to 10 times, creating additional jobs and economic opportunities. American's have a rich tradition of being resourceful, and the vast majority of new jobs since 1970 have been created by small businesses during the same period when corporations have been laying off millions of workers to increase corporate profits and executive compensation. The wealthy powerbrokers are sowing the seeds for worker rebellion.

Corporate executives must realize that in the long run, the prosperity of their companies are directly proportional to the prosperity of their workers. The American worker can become a formidable foe to corporate interests when pressed to the wall. Corporate America has been able to obtain pro-business special interest tax breaks and legislation only because the average voter had been relatively satisfied, and disinterested in political action. A dissatisfied electorate can be a formidable foe to politicians who they believe have lead to their economic misfortunes; and consequently, could elect a new breed of responsible politicians who would be more responsible to worker interests. Only short-sighted corporate executives would fail to recognize that keeping the American worker happy is good for business and long-term corporate health. (2012 – American workers continue to suffer lengthy periods of unemployment and underemployment while corporations sit on over $300 billion of cash and refuse to hire, juxtaposed against 3 million job openings for 25 million unemployed workers – with 14 million unemployed with no unemployment benefits. The vast majority of the 3 million job openings have requirements for new technological skills that the great majority of the unemployed do not possess).

THE CONCENTRATION AND CONTROL OF WEALTH (circa 1995, but true today)

Economics is taught in elite universities, yet all of these experts (who perpetually disagree with each other) have been unable to predict the actions of the economy with any measurable degree of accuracy. Much of the development of economic theories served to bolster the careers of so-called expert academicians, many of whom can not even balance their own checkbooks. Why not advance complex economic models and theories, such as Kensian economics, supply-side economics, Reaganomics, and other approaches, that when followed have created serious imbalances in the economy to benefit the wealthy.

When we eliminate the technical sounding jargon of theoretical economics, and apply common sense (as in dollars and cents), economic relationships can be explained in simple terms and concepts based on the law of cause and effect. There are four basic components of any economy; first, natural resources; second, manmade goods and services; third, distribution; and finally, value that is created by demand. The collective manipulations of the powerbrokers who control portions of these economic elements causes imbalances, and result in economy conditions that skews toward those who controls any of its elements. When any particular group controls the first three components, they develop a virtual monopoly on the fourth. Different political systems utilize laws to alter the natural relationship between these four elements of economy to shift wealth from its unprotected classes (the poor and consumer classes) to its protected classes (the economic and political powerful).

For many centuries, nations with formidable merchant and military shipping had the power to control global economic forces. In the recent past, the railroad, oil, automobile, and banking industries have exercised awesome control over the forces of the economy. Railroads gave way to air and trucking; oil became underminded by Arab excesses; the auto industry declined in the face of strong foreign competition; and unsound banking practices eroded depositor trust. The strength of most of these power industries of the past were primarily based on controlling the means of distribution. The new era of information processing has permitted technologically driven industries to make fortunes. Telecommunication, electronic media, and computer hardware/software advances permitted a quantum leap in information processing efficiency. Technology had its greatest impact in two areas; first in improving manufacturing quality and efficiency, and second in cybernetics, by providing almost instantaneous feedback on the effects of decision-making. Information technology provided business with the means for better internal control and simultaneously created new direct marketing opportunities through telephone and television. Information technology has produced new powerbrokers who will have an increasingly pervasive effect on influencing almost every aspect of our lives, and will gain a place among the traditional groups that have controlled the economy.

Yet, even without information technology, life can go on. It is not essential for bringing the basic necessities to doorsteps of the middleclass consumers. Food and shelter must still involve the human element, the pickers, builders, and drivers. While computers now assist in designing homes, and in ringing up prices at the supermarkets, people are still needed to build houses and to bring the food to the stores... at least for the foreseeable future. The human element (though to a lesser degree) is still required to keep the wheels of the economy going. Information technology by itself does not permit control of the economy, but assists those groups already exercising significant control to increase their ability to control economic factors.

The oil industry still exerts the greatest influence on the economy; however, health care, pharmaceuticals, information technology, telecommunications, and insurance are making great strides in affecting economic factors. Corporations that control significant portions of these industries will further increase their share of the economy, enabling them to dictate prices without regards for the natural effect of supply and demand. Back during the late 1960s and early 1970s, a major national labor union was almost able to position itself to greatly influence the price of food, except for the opposition of the fledgling United Farm Workers Union. Any group that is able to control a natural resource, labor, and distribution would be able to control prices, and consequently demand for that product.

Agricultural mechanization has reduced much of the labor intensiveness of food production; however, had that union national union succeeded to organize farm workers back in 1965, they would have controlled the labor of food production and transportation, two of the 3 economic elements needed to control supply and demand. And if representation of the supermarket checkers could have been wrestled from the AFL-CIO, then the chain of food production from the fields to the dining room table would have been complete. Presently, the greatest threat to low food prices is the growing elimination of small farmers, resulting in a concentration of control of natural resources in the hands of giant agribusiness conglomerates. Artificially manipulated food shortages are not too far off in the future. (2012 – one percent of the wealthy elites now own or control half of our national wealth. How many houses should anyone own? How many cars? Well as many as they want if they can afford it, but realistically they can only be in one house or one car at a time so why the greed?).

THE MAGIC OF SUPPLY AND DEMAND USING SMOKE AND MIRRORS (circa 1995, but true today)

he basis concept of supply and demand appear simple enough. A simple example would illustrate the effect of supply and demand. If ten people lived on an island, and the only source of food was fish, and there existed 10,000 fish, it is likely that the value of each fish would be such that fish could be used in barter to obtain other goods and services. However, if there were 10 people and only 100 fish, the value of each fish would increase such that people would desire to barter other goods and services to obtain fish. If there exist a limited supply of anything of value, its value will increase as a result of any increase in the number of persons having a demand. Taking the same example, if only 100 fish existed, but an abundance of fruit trees grew in the wild, then the value of fish would decrease because a demand for fish would decrease due to another food source.

What happens to confound the natural relationship between supply and demand is the effects of mass advertising. Sophisticated marketing techniques coupled with the vast influential power of high tech telecommunications has the effect of magic... the use of smoke and mirrors and slight of hand to fool the average consumer into making decisions based on deception and impulse. Creating desire (demand) based on slick techniques to convince American consumers that particular products are more valuable than they may be in reality. Thousands of companies have bought Into the concept that advertising on television and other mass media improves their market share. The tremendous cost of mass advertising is always passed on to the consumer in terms of higher product prices. Advertisers like to call this "value added", when in fact it is usually nothing more than waste and deceptive packaging on a grand scale to mislead the general public into buying products that are worth less than the price that they are charged. We all would be paying $500 for stainless steel toilet seats if the average American was as stupid as the government buyers. Fortunately, most Americans still possess some common sense.

Value is a fluctuation of human desire, an emotion that can be manipulated by cultural and societal influences. Scarcity of products desired by people will cause the value of those products to increase; however, scarcity for undesired products will not increase the value of unwanted products. Mass marketing is a method by which psychological suggestions are made within the context of societal and cultural dispositions to effect an emotional response pro or con pertaining to a particular product, service, or idea. Value is a subjective emotional perception that does not require factual content. Stocks and bonds, insurance, and other forms of speculative investments are primarily based on a perception of future value. Something with no intrinsic value can be marketed to create a demand. Fads come and go, just as people's desires peak and wane; consequently, value is sometimes an illusory and fleeting phenomenon. However, without value, there is not trade and thus no economy. Without value, there could be no wealth, and no way to amass the great fortunes people are willing to die for. (2012 – no wonder someone is always coming up with a new snake oil to sell to the public... a brief check of spam mail will show that clearly 90% of spam are also scams.)

WHAT DOES THE FUTURE HOLD? (circa 1995, but true today)

While the principles of solutions are basic and simple, the actual solutions to our problems are complicated by conflicting interests of people who stand to gain or lose whenever changes occur to upset the status quo, and consequently pose a potential threat to their economic power base. Solutions abound. Many things that can be better used; water can be a better source of energy; the value of gold, gems, and precious metals can become less speculative, and more realistic. An accurate assessment of supply and demand, utilizing data that is readily available to the general population is another method to provide economic predictability and security (so long as the data is easily verifiable and difficult to manipulate). Perhaps the time has come for a more reserved attitude toward evaluating performance, profit and loss ratios. How much is acceptable speculation; why do we take big changes to market products with little or no real value, just for the sake of wealth building?

Most world governments are in collusion with the international class of rich and powerful people. They send their nation's young men to die in wars to protect their national interest in Middle Eastern oil, and structure laws to benefit the rich while the commoners are going to bankruptcy. New ideas are suppressed or stolen In order for the status quo to get the most out of existing products; consequently, it usually takes 5-10 years for most new products to penetrate consumer markets, unless pushed by large corporate concerns. Sure, there are occasional success stories, like Bill Gates and Sam Walton. But how often does that happen? And will government ever send their sons and daughters to die in foreign wars for the sake of wealthy families? I don't think so. The traditional rich, and not the noveau riche still sit squarely in the saddle of economic and political power. There are some sure fire solutions to America's problems, only if enough average American would jump on the bandwagon. We need to take steps to safeguard inventors from having large corporations steal their patents by keeping them in court for their natural lives, or until the small inventor goes broke.

Other obstacles to progress include our dependency on oil and automobiles, defense industry big ticket items, and corporate greed. We need to improve the economy of all Americans, the poor, the middle-class, as well as the wealthy. We can not rely on our superpower role in improving world conditions until we first get our own house together. So often, history has shown that American intervention in the internal politics of foreign nations has usually made things worse because it creates additional chaos and upsets the basic infrastructure and relationships inside other countries.

Overpopulation in the developing world is a serious problem that threatens the viability of the human species on planet earth. It is a natural flow of evolutionary balance for mass deaths from various causes, including disease, insurrection, and starvation. Humanitarian aid to the world's hungry should be led by private charities who wish to express their religious conscience, and then only supplemented by government in the event of crisis. Too often, foreign aid to other nations only encourages and supports those who already weld political and economic power, with little going to assist the disheartened and downtrodden. Our attempt to solve all of the world's problems only compounds the long term effects on the environment, and by supporting one military or political faction over another, creates new enemies.

Education has always been pronounced as a foundational solution to all of society's ills. We now see a surplus of college grads taking menial jobs to survive. In the future, increase computing power will make our environment user friend, and will require little education to operate. In fact, schools, teaching, and learning will be subjected to new forms and competitive rules, becoming more personalized as computers become all pervasive. The power of television will be manifested in the new at-home schooling options, nurturing a new type of student who will redefine success, rightness, and will eliminate notions such as failure from our vocabulary. Education will become voluntary and not mandated by statute, as different classes of children become motivated to satisfy their own need for intellectual and social growth. Computer animation, virtual realty, and interactive television shows will create new avenues for recreation and sports.

Are technological advances solutions, placebos, or the poison to the social fabric of our future society? What do people do when their jobs are replaced by technology? Even jobs at McDonalds Hamburgers will be phased out someday. Computerizing world data to improve distribution of resources to areas of need, avoidance of overbuilding to maintain an ecological balance, and improving information accessibility could help to balance the rough spots that feed the causes of poverty, crime, and violence. Solutions must be found to constructively deal with the poor who are rapidly becoming the majority in America.

What part of the problems are rooted in governmental actions, and how can private concerns be further encouraged to provide viable solutions? How can we have peace within a context of environmentally sound industrial growth, while assisting in the course of world development, which would create new markets for American goods?

The social system will undergo profound changes due to changes in the workplace, government, communities, churches, attitudes about conformity, environmental pollution, HIV-AIDs and illness, world government, parenting, child abuse, childcare, family stress, grand-parenting, divorce, healthcare, gender and race relations, greed, and entertainment.

The political system will resist change, but there will be much pressure to institute computerized voting from home, and people will push for the replacement of politicians who owe their jobs to special interests lobbyists. Telephone, television, computer interactive voting will enable direct democratic participation in a real democracy. This will be possible due to instantaneous data analysis simultaneously across all time zones. We have too many laws, and a push will be made to eliminate an old and useless laws for each new law put on the books. Eventually, technocrats will replace politicians, with a mandate to serve the people's needs.

The governmental bureaucracy will shrink greatly as people will be able to take care of governmental matters directly from their computers, telephones, or televisions. Bureaucratic penalties will decrease as government redefines its mission. Instead of being the self propagating status quo machine, public servants will act as advocates for the people rights and interests. Government will no longer exempt itself and corporate industries from laws that are exercised on common citizens. The purpose of laws will stress justice and fairness, and not punishment and fines as ways to feed the criminal justice system.

Government will no longer suppress small businesses to keep corporations in control of the economy. The role of the police and courts will be to stay out of the business of law-abiding citizens, and to concentrate instead on the capturing and conviction of violent criminals and other societal predators. The funds for government will not come from income taxes, but from user taxes, so people may have a voice in how much government they really want through the frequency which it purchases public services.

These are not my ideas, but American ideals and the American way that was conceived by its revolutionary forefathers. It has been the crowning jewel of civilized men. The notion of democracy and freedom, fairness, equality in the eyes of God and men, justice, and free trade capitalism has attracted people from all over the world to emulate this great nation. It's time for America to set an shining example for the world to see, once again.

Chapter 6 – A World for all to enjoy (circa 2008)

As American and world citizens, we now find ourselves collectively hanging over an economic precipice that threatens to dislodge the current world order and to establish a new economic paradigm – another step closer toward the elusive one world order. As American elites and our government that represents their economic interests concentrate on gobbling up larger portions of the global economic wealth and its resources, our leaders are mired in inter-party bickering and political posturing, instead of focusing on a recovery plan for the good of all Americans. Believe it or not, the solution to the current economic threat to the civilized world is rather simple and straight forward as detailed on the following pages.

- Economic Principles:
- Economic activity equals GDP
- Market supply and demand forces impact economic activity
- Government policies and institutions impact economic activity
- Consumer confidence, ability and desire to purchase impact economic activity
- Non-liquid assets do not stimulate economic activity
- Greed is the motivating force behind unrestrained capitalism
- The value of Money, whether printed or digital is only as good as the acceptance of its value as collection on future debts, to discharge past debts and as a current medium of exchange – an IOU

- The monetary system is a house of cards based upon public confidence in the orderly and sustained value of the instruments of monetary exchange

If the cards at the foundation of the monetary/economic are weak, the house of cards will fall and all who are beholden to Humpty Dumpty won't be able to put him back together again. The present market reality:

- Stock market can collapse overnight, with no end in site.
- Credit locks up as banks run out of capital
- Psychological Principles:
- Investors lose confidence in stock market and pull out to avoid further erosion
- Depositors run on banks due to lost of confidence in the security of their money
- Fear results in accelerating withdrawal and heightening protectionism

Political Solutions:

- Stop the Wall Street skid by ignoring greedy stock broker complaints and immediately implement needed regulations against the creation of fraudulent products that have no value other than repackaging and bundling existing stocks
- Restore depositor confidence in the safety of their life savings in the banks
- Restore credit liquidity in the economy

- Average people are now beginning to understand that the economic system is predicated upon TRUST that the system is honest and fair. Having TRUST in the economic system creates public CONFIDENCE to deposit their life savings in banks and to invest their hard earned cash in the stock market.
- Out of control avarice and unchecked corruption in Wall Street and the banking industry has wiped out TRUST and CONFIDENCE of John & Jane Q. Public. As America slides and slumps, so follows the world.

Both TRUST and CONFIDENCE are based upon human psychological principles, thus the solutions must address perceived psychological threats to people's need for security sufficiently to calm people's anxieties. To restore TRUST and CONFIDENCE, the following are basic requirements:

- The federal government must promise to investigate and hold responsible the top CEOs, CFOs and COOs who were guilty of corruption, manipulation and fraud.
- The government must put in place adequate safeguards to prevent future fraudulent, predatory and illegal investment, brokerage, and banking practices.
- The federal government must show it is serious about "cleaning house" and ridding our economic system of fraud, corruption and Wall Street shell games.
- The government must temporarily step in to put the brakes on the monetary and stock market skid to stabilize markets, stop the run on banks and stabilize and reinvigorate the housing market by doing the following:

- Cash withdrawals from banks will be limited to $10,000 per week except commercial accounts utilized for payroll, business expenses, and capital improvements are exempt if used in the course of commerce. Already, ATM machines limit cash withdrawals to $500 per day, so people will see that if they still have access to their money, there shouldn't be a panic to get it out all at once. Why do we allow people to withdraw all of their money in one lump sum? It doesn't make any fiscal sense.
- FDIC's guarantee of deposits up to $250,000 per account should be permanent as the value of the long standing $100,000 has eroded with inflation and devaluation of the USD.
- Federal "bailouts" must not benefit the CEO's, CFO's and COO's of corporations such as AIG whose top executives stand to walk away with hundreds of millions of tax payer funds for their failures and possible conspiratorial and illegal acts. The acceptance of any corporation who applies for federal bail out funds must be preceded by the orderly resignation of its top executives, immediately the CEO and CFO – but retaining the COO during a time of transition.
- Homeowners on the brink of foreclosure must be given practical and manageable options to refinance their mortgages, such that their payments do not increase more than 5% per month this year and 7.5% per month in year 2 and 10% the next 3 years (based upon original pre-ARM adjusted rates). In exchange for this privilege, the FHA will guarantee the home loans as long as PITI is paid by homeowners. The savings to homeowners based upon

reduced monthly payments will accrue interest free and be added as a mortgage obligation repayment to the lenders when the houses are sold in the future.

- The government will become a temporary direct lender to banks with proper controls in place who lend to economically feasible commercial enterprises and to stringently qualified borrowers for home loans and large ticket items such as automobiles. Banks are expected to repay the Treasury 10% of their annual profits until these long-term loans are paid off. This is designed to immediately loosen up commercial and consumer credit.

- The government must not reward Wall Street hi-jinks, but instead lend (not give) funds to former Blue Chip firms that are now faced with the possibility of bankruptcy due to the irrational retrenchment of investors and customers based upon wanton fear – help is needed by General Motors who employ America's backbone.

- The federal government must promise to get to the bottom of any fraud, conspiracies and illegal schemes that got America and the world to this debacle, the worse since the Great Depression. Then the DOJ must deliver the goods and prosecute the greedy, dishonest and criminal culprits for all the world to see.

MORE TO COME LATER, BUT FIRST THINGS FIRST!

The U.S. government, as the international hegemonic power, can and does pretty much what it wants, as long as its power continues to appear legitimate to its electorate, and to its allies. In cases where American interests are served, the U.S. will go along with international conventions, but as soon as it feels its interests would be threatened, it will stand alone, without fear of reprisal or recrimination. Take for example the fact that the U.S. was the only dissenting vote in the U.N. on the latest ecological convention against greenhouse gases. Even if the U.S. was to sign such a convention, who is going to reprimand the U.S. government, or join in economic or military reprisals against America if it were to break the treaty? Especially in the current political climate, anyone, any group, or any state that is against the U.S. is likely to be seen, at the very least, as a terrorist sympathizer.

During WW2, the U.S. government earned its preeminence by proving it had the ability to engender patriotism and unquestioned support of government policies by its citizens during times of crisis. The U.S. also planted the seeds of economic imperialism by helping to rebuild Europe, Japan, and other post-colonial lands. If we look back at post-Nazi world history, most nations of the world are beholden to the U.S. for one thing or another, for American cash, industry, technology, liberation, modernization... something. Sure the CIA, as an instrument of U.S. foreign policy created conflict and helped to overthrow elected regimes that were viewed as hostile to U.S. interests, but that's what they're paid and sworn to do. Since the international community owes the U.S. so much, it is rare for them to gripe too much when America takes advantage from time to time, and tries to get the lion's share of what our world has to offer. Moreover, who dares to really challenge America? Just see what's happening to the Taliban now, what happened to Iraq a decade earlier, and what's likely to to happen to Saddam Hussein in a little while. No nation-state, group, or individuals in their right mind really wants to be on America's top "hit list", unless it has to do with music.

The bottom line is economic power, coupled with a powerful military, driven by technology, and supported by a patriotic (though often misinformed or somewhat brainless) citizenry, allows the U.S. to utilize various strategies, sometimes unfairly or illegitimately by international perspectives, to carry out policies that benefit those elite groups of domestic actors who exert the greatest influence on the government. When international situations threaten American hegemony, the U.S. government steps in to protect U.S. corporate interests and to protect the American economy, whether the cause of disequilibrium is oil prices, the nuclear arms race, or terrorism. And any benefits that the American power elite derives from the international system supposedly trickles down to the American masses, who as a group still enjoys one of the highest per capita incomes in the world (however, as the U.S. economy becomes more bifurcated, the poor more increasingly takes on attributes typically ascribed to Third World populations). Who can fight against all that? No one in their right mind would dare.

People or nation-states who are not of a right mind, who may even have legitimate complaints about economic sanctions or American policies, can only receive adequate redress when it gives in to playing the economic game by the international rules that has been developed by the United States of America, which ensures American dominance and hegemony.

ECONOMIC TRENDS

- Globalization
- Cultures of greed
- Corporate corruption
- Economic centralization
- Rise of oligarchs
- Food shortage pandemic
- Unemployment pandemic
- Bifurcation of income groups
- Outsourcing and jobs migration
- Devaluation of college education
- Skyrocketing price for food and nutrition
- Increased inflation and monetary devaluation
- Geometric increase in the price of oil and gasoline
- Secret conspiracy to collapse Internet periodically
- Secret manipulation of monetary and stock markets
- Parasitic, deceptive and fraudulent business practices
- Global reliance on Internet commerce & communication

CULTURAL TRENDS

- Sexploitation galore
- Increased ethnic and racial conflict
- Glamorization and worship of money
- Devaluation of life, both human and animals
- Accentuating "de facto" racial and ethnic discrimination
- Hierarchical social-economic ethnic and racial preferences

POLITICAL TRENDS

- Continued and heightened Middle-East conflicts
- Bureaucratic barriers and favoritism
- Government collusion and corruption
- News bias, unreliability and fabrication
- Growth of political "intranet" activist groups
- Rise in Islamic militancy, zealousness and extremism
- China becomes economic and military challenge to America
- State sponsored conspiracies with arms industry for conflict
- World divides into five political-cultural and economic "zones of influence"
- (comprised of Europe, Russia, China-Japan, and USA)
- Limited nuclear weapons usage in the Middle East by Israel and potentially uncontrolled global thermal nuclear war

TECHNOLOGICAL, SCIENTIFIC, GEOLOGICAL, METEORLOGIC TRENDS

- More reliant robotics
- Virtual reality integration
- Manned travel to Mars and Venus
- Significant meteor-asteroid impact
- Improved alternative energy utilization
- Stem cell research provide many new cures
- Accelerated depletion of petroleum reserves
- Artificial isolation of the energy of the "soul"
- Widespread use of "legalized recreational drugs"
- Increased meteorological instability and calamities
- Instrumental recordation of UFOs, ghosts, and ESP

- Increased environmental pollution and degradation
- Discovery of evidence of extraterrestrial civilizations
- Greater understanding of cosmology and universal forces

NEW WORLD ORDER TRENDS Explained

1.   ECONOMIC TRENDS
- Globalization
- removal of international trade barriers
- manipulation of supplies and market prices
- profits from labor exploitation and cost-efficiency
- global real time commodities and distribution tracking
- deeper Internet market penetration and commercialization
- Cultures of greed
- wealthy class is admired and revered
- "genius" becomes scientific AND economical term
- schools emphasize materialism and wealth building
- Corporate corruption
- fraudulent and unethical smoke and mirror bookkeeping
- stock manipulation to embellish CEOs versus shareholders
- exorbitant CEO salaries, perks, severance, & compensation
- Economic centralization
- rise of power and control of international oligarchs
- increase in concentration of wealth into smaller groups
- increase in monopolistic control of entire industries & fields
- increased price manipulation and artificial supply shortages
- commodities and manufactured goods.
- Food shortage pandemic

- destructive cyclical climatic changes cause widespread loss
- limited supplies are hoarded and high price gouging ensues
- human beings are "recycled" into nutrient paste and wafer
- waste products are added as "food fluff" in food products
- Unemployment pandemic
- new manufacturing techniques cause job obsolescence
- computerization eliminates need for human interfacing
- lacking cash cause greater self dependence, less service
- low education leads to low job demand and availability
- highly specialized education lead to niche employment
- Bifurcation of income groups
- the wealthy become super rich multi-billionaires
- the middle class shrinks with role to serve the wealthy
- the poor become miserable, impoverished and destitute
- the working poor are a notch above indentured servitude
- Global employment specialization and migration
- Jobs from all "portable" sectors migrate to low wage areas
- Asia becomes provider of low-wage labor for info & tech jobs
- Latin America becomes provider for manual labor assembly
- Europe becomes primary global financial-banking depository
- China-Japan become Asian regional financial-investment hub
- Africa becomes natural resources & mineral excavation center
- Antarctica becomes secondary source of fresh water resource
- Australia becomes major supplier of food; grain, meat, fruits.
- US remains primary source of new technology and research.

- Devaluation of college education
- non-technical degrees replace H. S. diploma as standard
- on-line education decreases need for professors/classrooms
- practical and technical training become higher valued degrees
- comprehensive testing and self-practicum in lieu of degrees
- Skyrocketing price for food and nutrition products
- natural cyclical food shortages vs. population explosion
- artificial shortages due to poor management and waste
- artificial shortages due to manipulation of supplies
- artificial distribution imbalances & price manipulation
- Increased inflation and monetary devaluation
- world currencies subject to recurrent hedge fund attacks
- oligarchs manipulate supplies to increase prices & profits
- IFM & World Bank negatively alter national economies
- international parasitic banking conspiracies
- accelerated oil prices due to various causes
- Geometric increase in the price of oil and gasoline
- accelerated oil prices due to increased consumption
- increased oil prices due to decreased oil reserves
- increased oil prices due to reduction in production
- Secret conspiracy to collapse Internet periodically
- to manipulate stock market trading & prices
- to cause distribution network imbalances for profit
- to disrupt banking functions, causing subterfuge
- for political leverage against targeted economies
- to blame cyber-terrorists for political gains
- to create economic & structural disorders and conflicts

- Secret manipulation of monetary and stock markets
- coordinated attacks against various currencies
- international bankers conspire to manipulate world currencies
- secret insider stock trading and conspiracies to defraud
- smoke and mirror accounting practices to hide embezzlement
- smoke and mirror accounting to manipulate "books"
- Parasitic, deceptive and fraudulent business practices
- deceptive and fraudulent accounting and bookkeeping
- shell corporations used to show false losses and hide profits
- price gouging when real or artificial shortages are created
- product substitutions & deliberate incorrect pricing
- Global reliance on Internet commerce & communication
- products are upc micro-chipped & real time I-net linked
- consumers' id by chip & real time linked to bank accounts
- paperless web-transactions with digital archiving
- subjected to regional power fluctuations & cyber-sabotage

2. CULTURAL TRENDS
- Sexploitation galore
- growth of child porn & prostitution, gay and bizarre deviancies
- exploitation of 3rd world as major I-net sex industry source
- sex-based product marketing to minors aged 10-17
- "protected" sexual activity is condoned for teens
- sex education extended to grade school (4th grade)
- Increased ethnic and racial conflict

- increased competition for government funds and programs
- "de facto" segregated neighborhoods abound
- transitional communities subjected to gang & racial conflict
- news media feeds on and sensationalizes ethnic/racial conflict
- growth of intolerance due to anti-Islamic sentiments
- growth of anti-Semitic sentiments
- growth of anti-Chinese sentiments
- increased ethnic power movements; black, Hispanic and white
- Glamorization and worship of money
- seeking wealth becomes the life purpose in most cultures
- people are respected and revered for amount of wealth
- poor people are considered baggage and outcast losers
- public sympathy for poverty wanes and charity decreases
- universal justification that people get what they deserve
- neo-caste system predominates most cultures as justification
- Devaluation of life, both human and animals
- value pegged to employment status and wealth
- elderly and poor get no respect, used to harvest organs
- external beauty glamorized, no respect for fat people
- uneducated get no respect and little employment opportunity
- homelessness exacerbated and moved to refugee camps
- insurance settlements pegged to person's net worth
- insurance settlements discount person's potential earnings
- bio-engineering enhancements have greater value
- genetic perfection becomes socialized eugenic goal
- Accentuating "de facto" racial and ethnic discrimination

- racial and ethnic enclaves abound
- conflict between enclaves increase; decrease travel
- separate ethnic neighborhood economies thrive
- schools become more segregated and problematic
- hierarchical social-economic ethnic and racial preferences

3. POLITICAL TRENDS
- Limited nuclear conflict
- Middle-East escalation; Israel uses tactical nukes on Iran
- No. Korea uses nukes; China responds with tactical nukes
- U.S. restrains from use of nukes to bring diplomacy
- Bureaucratic barriers and favoritism in private/public sectors
- insensitive automated phone tree/Internet driven agencies
- cronyism in hiring top administrative/executive positions
- middle-management cronyism & servitude to executives
- break down of civil service system by exceptions & loop holes
- Government collusion and corruption
- regulators enticed by private offerings and enhancements
- bureaucratic jobs are political payoffs and rewards
- sweetheart deals and exceptions given to well-connected
- corporate swindlers given broad playing field to cheat
- corporations use off-shore havens to avoid paying taxes
- multi-nations use shell game accounting to move profits
- banking industry has broad charges to rip off customers
- News bias, unreliability and fabrication
- news tailored to gain commercial endorsements/payments
- news greatly biased to support corporate status quo crooks

- news fabricated to persuade populace to hidden agendas
- news of unworthy but popular viewer topics such as sex scandals
- television media lose market share as global Internet
    - continue to become more popular
- Growth of political "intranet" activist groups
- grassroots activism through college webs and blogs increase
- cyber political activism increase geometrically
- cyber terrorism increase with new cyber bombs and attacks
- cyber "nuke" bombs used to attack Microsoft OS & IE browser
- Internet voting technology with bio-ID scan for on-line voting
- real time legislative review and public input via Internet links
- real time public opinion polls via various Internet sites/links
- Rise in Islamic militancy, zealousness and extremism
- Islamic reaction to American-Israeli Zionism increase
- religious extremism and anti-American sentiments rise
- anti-western, anti-modernism Islamic clerics are popularized
- Islamic terrorists explode WMDs on US and Israeli targets
- China becomes economic and military challenge to America
- US economy becomes dependent on Chinese production
- US defense firms approved for joint-ventures with PRC
- China seeks "parity" with US on all international fronts
- China seeks to absorb Taiwan over 20 years, or will attack
- China becomes major importer of American technology
- China becomes "respected" among world powers
- China agrees to larger global policing and humanitarian role
- State sponsored conspiracies with arms industry for conflict

- defense contractors and arms dealers conspire to create wars
- world leaders conspire with defense industry tycoons for deals
- Africa becomes latest battle ground for arms trader profits
- Africa is divided into various economic development zones
- African leaders are bought off by global oligarchs for land
- nations compete for new minerals and oil bonanza in Africa
- World divides into five political-economic "zones of influence"
- The "Big 4 of Europe, Russia, China-Japan, and USA.
- global terrorism is reduced to "manageable" levels globally
- moderate Islamic leaders and clerics rally for peace
- Africa's natural resources is divided up among the "Big 4"
- Uncontrolled nuclear war
- triggered by greed over Africa, nexus with Islamic terrorists
- Israel nukes Iran and Russia retaliates, backed by Islamic wealth
- all of the "Big 4" take heavy hits on cities and military sites
- nuclear war is over within hours, with 500 million people dead
- world is peaceful, as no nation has resources to invade others
- world famine ensues, with 500 million added radiation deaths
- global starvation is pandemic, with 2 billion barely subsisting
- average human lifespan decreases by 20 years
- additional 500 million die of disease, hygiene and starvation

- only GPS-based wireless Internet and cell phones operational
- societies devolve into ethnic/racial camps run by warlords
- wealthy people are hunted down and killed for their property
- surviving Internet is spotty, but allows new peace movement
- new societies emerge, pledged to peace and human progress

4. TECHNOLOGICAL, SCIENTIFIC, GEOLOGICAL, METEORLOGIC TRENDS
- More reliant robotics
- nano-robots become commercialized
- robotics widely used in retail, fast-food, and rubbish collection
- humanoid robots integrated into domestic-social environment
- medical robotics improve surgical and medical procedures
- Virtual reality integration
- portable VR headgear fully integrated to real time Internet
- VR addicts become new social problem
- human contact replaced by VR images
- 3-D VR enhancements allow real time customer interactions
- 3-D VR sexual encounters are the rave for safe sex
- Manned travel to Mars and Venus
- new rocket propellant coupled with photon engines
- new process to create water and oxygen for long trips
- lighter and stronger materials for spaceship structure/shell
- new high-nutrient tasty dehydrated food logs developed

- in-space travel speeds increased 4 folds to 200,000 mph
- semi-sleep suspended animation for long trips developed
- Significant meteor-asteroid impact
- meteor storm w/2 mile wide meteors impact oceans and land
- major ocean front cities inundated by huge tidal waves
- major 9.0 earthquakes result from land impacts, level cities
- major dust storms created, causing 2 year temperature drop
- negative effect on farming, grazing, and food production
- 500 million people die from consequences of meteor impacts
- Improved alternative energy utilization
- oceanic wave power generation plants abound
- solar collectors increase 10 fold in power output
- fuel cells/steam engine hybrids reduce gasoline usage
- planetary gravitation field is tapped for electrical energy
- perpetual energy machines used to power homes
- mini-wind power generators designed into all vehicles
- bio-mass and bio-chemical energy production improved
- Stem cell research provide many new cures
- most degenerative diseases cured by stem cell regeneration
- cancer is cured through surgery and stem cell regeneration
- nerve regeneration through stem cell stews cure paralysis
- Accelerated depletion of petroleum reserves
- increased global development drastically reduces reserves
- many supposed reserves are found to be dry wells
- oil deposit discovery peaks
- Artificial isolation of the energy of the "soul"
- energy shield "death chamber" retains "soul" within chamber

- "soul" image measurable, digitized and image made visible
- great progress on communicating with "soul" of dead persons
- Widespread use of "legalized recreational drugs"
- new non-addictive recreational drugs sold OTC by RX firms
- street drugs lose attractiveness, replaced by new synthetics
- recreational synthetics permit enhanced human performances
- Increased meteorological instability and calamities
- earth enters 200 year meteorological extremism cycle
- category 4-5 hurricanes, tornadoes and typhoons triple
- 6.5 – 8.0 magnitude earthquakes quadruple
- persistent droughts, alternating with torrential rains destroys
- "el Nino" effect increases 200 percent in northern hemisphere
- increased volcanism by 5 folds, polluting jet stream and air
- Instrumental recordation of UFOs, ghosts, and ESP
- world governments admit to covering up UFO evidence
- new instruments developed to measure one-dimensional shift
- parallel worlds detected within current time/space continuum
- ESP booster relays permit brainwave transmission/reception
- ghosts are isolated and communicate through technology
- Increased environmental pollution and degradation
- increased global development, population and waste pollutes
- development of rain purification systems for drinkable water
- oceanic desalination increase potable water supplies

- most rivers and lakes become polluted beyond safety
- water recycling technology provides 90% of recoverable water
- Discovery of evidence of extraterrestrial civilizations
- archeological digs on moon and Mars indicated civilizations
- DNA recovered on moon and Mars mirrors early earth life
- theologists and scientists surmise Mars was original "Eden"
- "alien high-technology" discovered along with historical record
- extraterrestrial space crafts discovered on moon and Mars
- ET's present themselves, living in hollow center "eye" of earth
- organized world religions falters to adjust to new reality
- Greater understanding of cosmology and universal forces
- universal formula relates all forces large and small
- universal formula relates all matter, space and anti-matter
- universal formula relates nothingness and infinity
- universal formula relates time, prophecy, and fulfillment
- universal formula relates galaxies, Big Bang, and renewal
- increased evidence of dynamic cosmologic destruction
- universal mathematical formula applied to cosmology
- actual beginning of our universe is calculated within 100K yrs

A VISION OF SUSTAINABLE NATIONAL AND GLOBAL FIXES

Why does the majority of our world's population continue to be imprisoned by conflict, disease, starvation, poverty and misery? What are worthwhile pursuits which could correct the injustices and resource imbalances that are caused by institutionalized greed, corporate and political corruption, elitism, and prejudice? What comprehensive vision must be universally recognized in order for international policy makers to cooperate on joint ventures that can save our world from our worsening development and population pressure? Will things ever change for the better?

Overcoming the five human flaws:

Five fundamental flaws have evolved in the human psyche through the interaction of genetic predisposition and cultural orientation, particularly through the spread of western civilization and values. These major flaws have enabled the elites, predators, madmen, tyrants, and war mongers to rule the meek and manipulate the beliefs and actions of the Ignorant. Perhaps these five human flaws were evolutionary strengths during the early stages of human evolution into communities, cultures, civilizations and more recently into nation-states, because it permitted the unification of the efforts of many toward greater accomplishments that surpass individual capacities. Or perhaps these five flaws have marred the human race and has taken us down a path to certain mutual destruction, which the trends toward the event horizon appear to confirm.

These five flaws are 1) value defined as winning vs. losing; 2) the global paradigm of greed and wealth building; 3) the worship of efficiency; 4) the overemphasis on productivity; and 5) the cheapening of humanity. A discussion of each of these human flaws in the context of modern times exposes the destructive nature of baser human instincts that may have benefited human survival eons ago, but now serve only to alienate, exploit, and enslave humanity to a path that leads only to eventual extinction.

1)   Children learn early on during the social and cultural indoctrination period during school years the importance of winning vs. losing. The grading system celebrates the top ten percent as winners, and consequently the remaining 90% are losers – also rans. No wonder an alarming number of teenagers drop out of a school system that is based upon punitive measures that rob individuals their basic sense of self-worth, while attempting to force conformity. Perhaps the top 10% aren't so much winners, but are instead the highest level conformist and maintainers of social standards... who teachers often tout as our nation's future leaders. Certainly, as disproportionate number of those who succeed in the academic track join the ranks of educators, professionals, bureaucrats, managers, and law makers, whose primary motive is to enforce social order and to pass on the values of organizations that support social order. Those who maintain social norms and conform to society's laws and values receive its rewards as middle-class careerists, and those who fail to encapsulate educational indoctrination fill the ranks of criminality and marginal subgroups that lurk in the background, not sharing in social economic prosperity. Winners are those who are defined by their higher

educational and economic levels, and losers are those who slide into the lower pits of society.

What if the educational system were to instill a sense of self-worth and to encourage the development of everyone's innate desire to discover and learn? These certainly are very innate human qualities that are naturally exhibited by toddlers and young children before the educational system's punitive paradigm attempts to transform individuals into sheep and cattle. Every human being deserves the opportunity to believe in the value of their unique individual traits – personality, talents, skills, aptitudes, attitudes, and beliefs. It is an basic injustice for social institutions and government to impose a cookie cutter to our young and impressionable. It is abundantly clear that adult members of extremist groups have modeled themselves during their formative years among extremists, such as gangs, racists, and terrorists.

What if the value of the Olympic experience were to celebrate the human potential, instead of medals? Then all could be winners, and not just the three in any event. What is so important about standing on the top podium? Is that view of the world significantly better than that of the audience? The audience sees an individual standing on a podium, listening to his/her national anthem. The individual on the platform is blinding by a sea of unrecognizable faces and the glare of television lights and camera flashes. Who sees the true reality? Are those in the audience envious of the one on the podium? Do they feel that particular individual is a true winner for accomplishing a basically worthless and inane physical feats? Certainly many in the audience who have been brainwashed and indoctrinated by the educational and marketing institutions are suckers to admire those who can achieve apparently superhuman feats that they themselves are incapable of doing. That makes those members of the audience less than winners – it makes them losers and spectators in life... not its primarily celebrated participants.

If we put so much value into the physical accomplishment of superhuman feats and setting records for human performance, then why is there so much resistance to the enhancement of human capacity and potential performance through the use of drugs and genetic engineering? If we really want to push the envelop of human development and evolution, let's apply genetics and science to enhance human potential. Would that be cheating? Certainly not. There is no such thing as fairness in this world. Ask the person who is homeless about fairness, and you will receive an honest response. Ask the rich person who inherited wealth the same question, and no doubt fairness is not an issue. If winning continues to be so highly regarded, then people should be allowed to make their own personal decisions on what they are willing to do to win, which should no more be restricted than society is willing to restrict the tactics and performance of the wealthy, who use unfair business practices to monopolize entire industries to drive out their competitors, to enable them to control the market and dictate prices, such as what has happened in the oil, defense, media, and banking industries.

If we analyze the true value of winning, it is no more than a marketing tool to validate and celebrate the few in order to increase the corporate profits of sponsors who understand the need of the masses of losers who need to identify themselves with a winning team, nation, or individuals. Winning is just another marketing gimmick, no more and no less. People should be encouraged to participate in life, and not simply to view their dreams vicariously through the accomplishment of others, who the manipulators of social values and standards have decided are good for profits. Every human being has inherent value and the potential to achieve great things within the limits of their talents and resources. Each individual possess innate talents that has the potential to give great joy to oneself and to those around them, when socially conditioned judgment is suspended.

The concept of winning versus losing no longer has a constructive role in modern society. Perhaps in primitive human cultures, the winners were those who had the physical capacity to hunt down the game that gave their tribes another week of sustenance. Perhaps in early civilizations, the winners were the heartless murderers who defeated other tribes and the defenseless, such has been recorded throughout human history in the conquest of the weak by supposed great civilizations – the Romans, Mongols, and Greeks. How many women, infants, children, aged, and defenseless had to die so these supposed great conquerors – winners – could enslave and rule over people who never needed them nor invited them into their lands?

The native tribes in the America's were seats of great primarily peaceful civilizations whose cultures and values were in consonance with the earth and the natural order. They did not place winning as the highest societal goal, but instead valued true social order that was earned through self-sacrifice for the community benefit. They realized that the survival of their tribes and people depended upon cooperation, whether in the pursuit of game or in agriculture. Could such a peaceful, non-destructive, non-exploitive and non-competitive paradigm benefit people today?

Certainly far more than the winner takes all paradigm that currently rules the human psyche of the international elites and wealthy carpetbaggers who enforce poverty on the world in order to strip it of its natural resources for the profit of the few, to the misery of the great faceless masses. What if it's okay not to strive to be the winner? What type of society would we have? We would likely have a world filled with people who go about their lives, not concerned about winning, but naturally pursuing their personal interests without regard for winning or losing. Without a definition of winning and losing, people would simply act and try to accomplish their personal potential in activities that interest them. Golfers could feel good about shooting a round of 100 because the course, weather and companionship was wonderful and they finished the course within the number of shots set by thier personal goals. But instead, people tend to fall into the trap of comparing their scores to those of others, and worse yet to those of the pros. So instead of being the winners that they are, who should not need validation, especially in inconsequential and inane tasks, they instead punish themselves with feelings of inadequacy and failure. Then why bother to partake in stupid things where the certain outcome is negative and detrimental to one's self-worth?

The danger in people rejecting the concepts of winning and losing is the empowerment of the human spirit! How would it feel to do something for the sheer joy of doing it, and not as a pursuit of a score or standard arbitrarily set by others, who have died long ago? How would this change the marketing strategy of major corporations? Would people stop watching television and all head for the ball parks, golf courses, and bowling alleys? Not likely for a generation raised on watching cartoons and television sports, and more recently on violent video games. To the participant, it's an achievement. To the viewer, it's entertainment. To the sponsors, it's profits. We don't need winners and losers, because the games are entertaining enough, and consequently, everyone can just be themselves without regards for winning or losing, or being superior or inferior. People can begin to respect the fact that we are all different and have innate value as participants in the games of life.

When cultures, nations, and peoples accept the vast differences and variations that exists among individuals of all walks of life, who pursue and value different aspects of reality and religion, then perhaps the human race would stand an improved chance for continued evolution and prosperity. The winner takes all paradigm certainly will only encourage the failure of the human race. Does winning have any value besides what people make of it in their culture? In the vast universe of a hundred billion billion stars, which one is the best? Which star is a winner that stands alone above the rest? And why, if there could be such a star, would it even matter, or should it matter. Each star is uniquely different from the rest, as no two galaxies or planets are the same. As vast as each grain of sand in the expansive sky, the uniqueness of each star contributes to the beauty of the night, as each individual human being has the potential to add to the beautiful phenomenon that is life itself.

2)   The global paradigm of greed and wealth building has set into place an insidious and far reaching system of exploitation and global destruction unprecedented in the annals of human endeavor. In the pursuit of wealth, the ecosystem is being destroyed. In the pursuit of wealth, unique cultures have been and are being destroyed. In the pursuit of wealth, people commit

crimes and murder. In the pursuit of wealth, nations have gone on wars of conquest. In the pursuit of wealth, a singular world government is becoming the goal of oligarchs and multinational corporations. In the pursuit of wealth, the inherent value of human beings has been relegated to that of cheap laborers and consumers, as integrated parts of the global money making machine, owned by the rich.

What is the addictive appeal of money? When is enough, enough? A person can eat only one meal at a time, be in one room in one house at a time, drive one vehicle at a time, and wear one set of clothes at a time. Does owning and hoarding more clothes, property and material things make a person more valuable as a human being? If their wealth is built upon indentured servitude of others, low-paid marginally surviving workers who toil under horrendous conditions, or due to their manufacturing processes wildlife and habitat are destroyed, do the profits of wealth-building make the wealthy better people? And why should wealth building be an admirable goal and the rich held up on high pedestals when their rise to the top was already on the bent backs of the working poor? Unfortunately, it appears the lure of money is so universal that most people, no matter where and in what nation, would be willing to sacrifice their souls for money.

3) The worship of efficiency is no more than human exploitation by corporate big wigs who want to maximize profits by any means possible. People are driven to work harder and longer hours, to be more efficient producers in order to minimize labor costs while maximizing productivity. Cheaper labor markets are exploited where laws do not exist to provide basic protections to workers, and the working poor in western nations can not compete

to sustain their miserable low-paying jobs, not to mention the better paying jobs that are rapidly vanishing in the workplace. Corporations are only concerned about profit margin and global competitiveness, and social responsibility counts only when charitable contributions lower their corporate tax burden. Consequently, a twisted capitalism has become the product of corporate greed and corruption, where the four money-making principles that rule CEO decision making

have become maximize profits by minimizing operational costs primarily by increasing efficiency through downsizing and outsourcing to cheaper labor markets. And whenever possible, charge the highest margin the market will permit between the cost of supplies and consumption price.

Corporations achieve market advantage through mergers, hostile takeovers, and acquisitions that centralize the control of supplies and distribution to permit monopolistic control of the marketplace. Gaining such control is considered the hallmark of operational efficiency because the maximum price can be obtained for supplies that are controlled, or the minimum price can be paid to supplies they do not control, if they can control distribution. The object of pricing efficiency is to pay the least possible for supplies that must be purchased, charge the maximum for supplies that are owned, brokered, or sold, pay the minimum for labor and other operational costs. What happened to the socially responsible paradigm capitalism, of producing or providing products or services that serve real consumer needs (not artificial needs created through slick and deceptive marketing ploys), and charging reasonable prices where workers who produce the products can themselves afford to be the consumers of the products of their labor? Perhaps that paradigm is falling to the wayside.

4)   The overemphasis on productivity is based upon modern euphemistic restatement and enforcement of indentured servitude, or border-lined slavery. Cheap laborers, particularly in developing nations who work for relatively little enable multi-national corporations to substitute low-pay labor markets for the higher cost labor in developed nations, thereby exacerbating the potential unemployment quandary. As robotics and technologies continue to make great leaps forward, most jobs now reliant to some degree on human participation will eventually vanish because machines will be more productive. When the power goes off, civilization will instantaneously fall back into the stone age, and people will degenerate into warring tribes run by feudal lords.

5)   The cheapening of humanity has resulted from modern day globalization due to the utility value of cheap laborers defining the net worth of human beings according to their productivity rate in proportion to corporate profits. In the evolution of pre-modernity, cultures valued human life as of inherent value subject only to the whims of god(s). To each civilization, rulers and the nobility ruled their subjects in accordance to the intrinsic value of human life – that each human being was as basically as valuable as another... that life was sacred because it was created by a higher being. In our modern money driven world, the worth of people has become relegated to their purchasing power.

Why should drug addicted heirs of great family fortunes be held in higher esteem than those afflicted among the poor? Why still should irresponsible and brash kids of the elites be considered any better than those of commoners? Why are people with more money valued higher than those with less? Shouldn't a person who works hard in an honest back-breaking job to put food on his family's table be valued at least as highly as the billionaire's spoiled brat whose arrogance justifies bad temperament and low morals? Not in the world we live in. The news media and movies have made the general public into zombies, worshipers of those who are used to shape public opinion and norms, while behind the scenes the truly powerful and wealthy are hoarded their money off into secret off shore bank accounts to evade taxes.

All people have intrinsic value – that of being living, sentient beings who are capable of independent thought and actions (though often not expressed as such). Why do so many feel they need to be led? Because too many desire to lead. So periodically, people follow madmen whose own self-aggrandizement justifies their psychotic ethnic cleansing campaigns whether against Jews, Moslems, Christians, native tribes, or "savages".
The ultimate fault of the human species is intolerance, without which people would be more able to live among each other in peace and mutual respect And with tolerance, people would recognize that everyone and all life possess intrinsic value.

Ranking second on the short list of human frailties, is greed. Greed is a two edge sword that can cut stone into great civilization or cut deep into the collective soul of entire races of people and nations. While greed allows the accumulation of great amounts that are necessary to build great monuments and the dreams of inventors, too often its uses are to fund human suffering among the faceless masses. Drug dealers make fortunes as millions become permanently addicted to the destructive nature of narcotics and other street drugs. But pharmaceutical conglomerates also exploit human misery by supplying prescription drugs at high prices, often with negative health and economic side effects. Arms merchants earn billions through the black market arms trade as their agents foment conflict and warfare in third world nations, but weapons manufacturers make hundreds of billions of dollars in legitimate profits once the smaller smoldering conflicts can justify a full scale war in the Third World. And behind most of the economic activities of the world are investment bankers, who fund anything that makes a quick buck, whether it would be trading in legal or illegal drugs, legal or illegal weapons, wars or terrorism. Money makes the world go around, and in the global economy, it is the grease that keeps the economic wheels of the global elites turning.

Will a "perfect world" ever be possible? Certainly the world of the 3rd millennium appears to be more progressive than that of the first century, right? The facts clearly show the world contains more hungry people now than ever before in human history, and the percentage of the poor has never been higher – all juxtaposed against the rapidly rising wealth of the top ten percent, and especially the top one tenth of one percent of the global economic elites. Don't be fooled by all the horns and whistles, the glitz and glamour and shifting mirrors. The world is not a better place than it was 2,000 years ago, and perhaps not even 5,000 years ago or 10,000 years ago. Modern humanity continues to be subject to natural calamities, tornadoes, hurricanes, floods, earthquakes, droughts and pandemic diseases. Modern humanity continues to be plagued by religious intolerance, poverty, starvation, and armed conflict that results in massive deaths. Modern humanity has the same face of ancient humanity, only with more scars, as people continue to follow madmen, tyrants, and lunatics not too distant in kind from Adolph Hitler.

If we were to define a "perfect world" as one where disease has been conquered, starvation does not exist, and everyone acts responsibly within their communities to foster tolerance and peaceful interactions, does the world have the capacity to support the development of a "perfect world"? The answer is "yes" and "no" for the following reasons:

1.   Yes because it is human nature to strive for a sense of belonging, while feeling their individual existence is of value to those who they love, who love them. And no because people are naturally intolerant due to fear of the unknown and unfamiliar. People's daily lives are a constant interplay between the forces of love and fear. Do workers love their jobs or fear their bosses? Do spouses refrain from infidelity because they love each other or from fear of the consequences of getting caught in an intimate relationship with another? Do students love to learn mandatory subjects to qualify for a degree, or from fear of failure? Usually, people compromise and neither do they do only those things that they cherish, nor do they refrain from doing those things they loath.

2.   No, because a perfect world will only be possible when people's desire for truth and love far exceeds their propensities for fear and greed (which is oftentimes an overcompensation for the fear of unpredictability). In a perfect world, variety and abundance would rule the day as fear would become extinct. People would be motivated by a desire to seek knowledge as a pleasure of growth and development, and not for any need for validation or permission of the government to work

in any career. The sheer intrinsic joy of discovery and learning are strong allies against intimidation of fear.

Sir Winston Churchill once articulated while staring down the barrel of the NAZI war machine stated to his countrymen, "There is nothing to fear, but fear itself." An the acts of countless heroes were the results of men who overcame their fear of fear in order to make great human sacrifices for the greater good. Certainly confronting fear and overcoming it makes us stronger people.

Is a perfect world likely? Not until world population, development, pollution, disease, and starvation are brought under control and an equilibrium is established.   And that is not likely to happen anytime soon, but we must not take our eyes off the target, otherwise it is never going to happen for another thousand years or maybe just never.   And what's the worse outcome that can happen if the world's leaders and peoples focus on building an ideal harmonious world?   Not failure as anything less will be progress toward a BETTER WORLD. Let it begin NOW! It's really worth it. Otherwise, the world will continue to SUCK!

Note: All images downloaded from Internet public domain

www.ingramcontent.com/pod-product-compliance
Lightning Source LLC
Chambersburg PA
CBHW060249290526
45789CB00001B/263